MONASTIC WISDOM SERIES: NUMBER FOURTEEN

Gonzalo Maria Fernández, ocso

God Alone

A Spiritual Biography of
Blessed Rafael Arnáiz Barón

T0204278

MONASTIC WISDOM SERIES

Patrick Hart, ocso, General Editor

Advisory Board

Michael Casey, ocso	Terrence Kardong, osb
Lawrence S. Cunningham	Kathleen Norris
Bonnie Thurston	Miriam Pollard, ocso

MONASTIC WISDOM SERIES: NUMBER FOURTEEN

God Alone

A Spiritual Biography of Blessed Rafael Arnáiz Barón

by

Gonzalo Maria Fernández, ocso

Translated with a Note by
Hugh McCaffery, ocso

Edited by
Kathleen O'Neill, ocso

CISTERCIAN PUBLICATIONS
Kalamazoo, Michigan

Originally published as
El Beato Hermano Rafael: Biografía espiritual
by Editorial Catolica, Madrid, 1984

Cistercian Publications

Editorial Offices
The Institute of Cistercian Studies
Western Michigan University
Kalamazoo, Michigan 49008-5415
cistpub@wmich.edu

The work of Cistercian Publications is made possible in part by support from Western Michigan University to The Institute of Cistercian Studies.

Library of Congress Cataloging-in-Publication Data

Fernandez, Gonzalo Maria.
  [Hermano Rafael. English]
  God alone : a spiritual biography of Blessed Rafael Arnaiz Baron
/ by Gonzalo Maria Fernandez ; translated with a note by
Hugh McCaffery.
     p.   cm. — (Monastic wisdom series ; no. 14)
  ISBN 978-0-87907-014-4
  1. Arnáiz Barón, Rafael, 1911–1938.   2. Trappists—Spain—
Biography.   I. Title.

BX4705.A732F4713   2007
271'.1202--dc22
[B]   2007051283

Printed in the United States of America.

TABLE OF CONTENTS

PREFACE TO THE FIRST EDITION

To no one on earth has it been granted to gaze at heaven through an open door. Nonetheless, one may, perhaps, attempt to catch a glimpse of it through the chinks that open up in the Cistercian monastery of San Isidoro de Dueñas. When, after the chanting of each Psalm, the monks bow profoundly and say, "Glory be to the Father and to the Son and to the Holy Spirit," one gets some idea of what the heavenly chant of praise to the Lord is like.

The book you are reading comes from that monastery. It is an exceptionally rare book. Indeed, I am not sure that it is merely a book. It is rather a modicum of mystery. Father Gonzalo has attempted the impossible: to write an account of a mystical matter. Mysticism carries with it, even linguistically, the sense of something hidden, impenetrable. Mystical—from the same Greek root as *mysterious*—is what can neither be said nor shared, while a book is a means of communication: its ultimate purpose is that it be read.

Obviously, Father Gonzalo has not achieved the impossible. By reading this work one cannot really "know" the mind and heart of Brother Rafael. But one can gain understanding of and love for him; maybe envy him also. Then, one will no longer understand oneself completely, and thereby one will have come closer to the Truth.

Father Gonzalo has written an objective, scientific and strictly systematic work. With deep knowledge of his subject and perceptible devotion, he has dealt with the rich and delicate material that comprises Brother Rafael's original writings. And Father Gonzalo has definitely achieved his purpose. He has brought off something surprising and unexpected. The objective narrative so penetrates the mind and heart of the reader that it melts and merges with the reader's own living. This, of course, was made possible only because the author had already given himself completely to the same kind of living. Otherwise there would have been no such result.

This work does truly and successfully convey the spiritual development of the one whose story it is. This development was more complicated than that of most others, not just because of its quality, but also because of the frequent shuttling that he had to go through: entry at his La Trappe, returning to the outside world, another attempt at monastic life, etc. Although all of this could be found in earlier publications, it is recounted here with very great clarity, and above all with the sensitivity that the matter demands, the implicit psychological analysis of which is both extremely interesting and free from pedantry and dishonesty.

Biographies, as a rule, are written about the "top people," noted participants in historical events of far-reaching significance. Their biographers enjoy the benefit that accrues to their efforts from the fame of those whose lives they write about. No matter how obscure and complex the personalities of such active people may be, it is always easier to write their biographies than it is to put together the "spiritual biography" of a contemplative monk, which makes the work of the author of this book doubly admirable.

Readers who begin to turn the pages of this short book are warned that they will not find in it even one single piece of literary criticism. True, Saint John of the Cross—the greatest poet in Spanish literature!—is often quoted, but he is not credited with any influence whatever over either the thought or the writing of Brother Rafael. Friar John and Brother Rafael did but follow parallel paths under the impulse of the same inspiring: that of the Spirit who transcends everything.

Once taken up, this book has simply got to be read, read carefully and completely. Possibly at the end one may not have grasped its ultimate meaning. But, after all, this book is meant not so much to be understood as to be lived, to the extent of the grace granted to the reader by God.

—Patricio Pemán

PREFACE TO THE SECOND EDITION

Fray Luis de León wrote that he had come to know Mother Teresa of Jesus through her writings and through her daughters. And, in fact, in her writings she reveals herself and the wealth of her spiritual experience, her sure feel for Gospel values, her outstanding psychological insight, her never-failing charm, and the genius of her self-expression; and the charm of the Holy Mother lives on in her Carmelite Sisters. Something similar can be said of Brother Rafael: we can come to know him through his writings and through his fellow Trappists. In his writings he presents himself as a Christian and a man of prayer, as someone with a monastic vocation both inside and outside the cloister, and he captivates the reader with the conversation of a human being marvelously alive. Likewise one discovers a calling and a mentality like his in the Trappists of San Isidore de Deuñas. Once across the railway tracks on the way to the monastery, one finds oneself in another world with another language. Visitors can be impressed by the peace, by the good order, by the liturgical chant; Rafael and the monks have also and above all found God in their La Trappe. "God alone fully satisfies" (Saint Teresa). "God alone" (Rafael). This precious book tells becomingly and quietly, with depth and unction, what Rafael found.

In 1988 the *Complete Works* of Brother Rafael were published by the Monte Carmelo Editions of Burgos and by the Monastery of Dueñas. They had already appeared in part in *A Secret of La Trappe* (Brother Rafael, 1944) by his uncle, the Duke of Maqueda, and in the compilation made by his mother, *Writings and Biographical Details about Brother Mary Rafael Arnáiz Barón, Trappist Monk* (1947). These writings were like a loud knocking that concentrated the minds of Christians on someone both secluded and splendid. The resulting sound wave has kept spreading to places and persons ever since. The present work was written by the

present Abbot of Rafael's La Trappe, Dom Gonzalo M. Fernández. It is an expertly planned guide that simply and perceptively
traces in successive stages the writings, the chronology and, as
far as possible, the story of Rafael's soul. It is written with exact
knowledge, with fellow-feeling for a monk of the same spiritual
lineage, together with the simplicity proper to a monk interiorly
detached, and yet a partner in vocation and experience. Rafael,
like Saint Teresa, does indeed live on in his writings and in his
brother monks.

Rafael was beatified by John Paul II, in the piazza of Saint
Peter's, Rome, on September 27, 1992. How great was the reveren-
tial joy we all experienced when the portrait of the lowly Trappist
oblate appeared on the tapestry hanging from the balcony of the
loggia of the Vatican Basilica amid the thunderous applause of
the numberless crowd! Once again God was publicly exalting
the lowly. This new edition of the book makes its appearance
subsequent to Rafael's beatification, in the light of which its pages
gain fresh splendor and speak to us with even greater eloquence.
While a seminarian at Avila, I often used to visit the country dis-
trict around Pedrosillo from which Rafael came straight to his La
Trappe. As bishop of Palencia, I had the privilege of making the
ritual request for Brother Rafael's beatification during the solemn
ceremony of September 27 in Rome. In our diocese we benefit
by the God-given grace of this monastery; I am delighted with
the friendship of Father Abbot Gonzalo; it has been a pleasure
to write these few lines.

—Ricardo Blásquez, Bishop of Palencia, Palencia, Spain

TRANSLATOR'S NOTE

This translation has been done with Dom Gonzalo's express permission, and with my Abbot's generous encouragement.

Three words used in the course of the narrative would seem to call for explanation in the case of a reader less well-acquainted with monastic and Cistercian terminology.

TRAPPIST: a Cistercian monk or nun belonging to the reform among Cistercians that originated during the second-half of the seventeenth century at the Cistercian monastery of La Trappe in Normandy. During the French Revolution all the religious houses in France were suppressed by the National Assembly, so a group of monks from La Trappe set up a monastery in Switzerland. From then on, there was a universal tendency to call these Cistercians and their successors "Trappists."

OBLATE: a member of a Trappist-Cistercian community who shares its monastic life in the measure appointed by the Superior, and is not bound by the vows taken in the Order.

COWL: The Trappist-Cistercian cowl is a white, ankle-length over-garment with long, wide sleeves; the cowl of monks (but not that of nuns) is topped by a hood of the same material. It is regarded as *the* garment of fully-professed monks and nuns.

—Hugh McCaffery, ocso, Mount Melleray Abbey,
Cappoquin, Waterford, Ireland

GENERAL EDITOR'S NOTE

After this biography was written, *Cistercian Studies Quarterly* began to publish serially the monastic writings of Brother Rafael. These were translated by Sister Juanita Colon and Sister Charles Longuemare of Mount Saint Mary's Abbey, Wrentham, Massachusetts. Sister Juanita began the project and wrote an introduction to the first three essays, before her poor health prevented her from continuing the work. Following her death, Sister Charles picked up the work and translated the following four sections. These seven offprints were published in *CSQ* from 1998 to 2003, illustrated by sixteen line drawings by Brother Rafael. In 2003 these offprints were gathered together to form a *CSQ* reprint. Copies of this 170-page paperback book, *Life and Writings of Blessed Rafael Arnáiz Barón* are still available from Cistercian Studies Quarterly, O.L. Mississippi Abbey, 8400 Abbey Hill Ln, Dubuque IA 52003-9501.

—Patrick Hart, ocso / Abbey of Gethsemani,
3642 Monks Rd., Trappist, KY 40051

INTRODUCTION

Blessed Rafael's own writings are undoubtedly the most important and direct source for a spiritual biography of him. Owing to various circumstances, both interior and exterior in his life, as will become evident in the course of this book, Rafael wrote quite a lot.

Apart from a few letters he wrote in early childhood, it can be said that all his writings can be classified as "spiritual writing," since they disclose the tendency of his prayer. They are not in fact doctrinal or didactic; they are writings that came from his heart and mind, a wonderful upsurge of prayer as he recalls happenings in his life. Rafael himself says so in some of his letters and short pieces: "As soon as I put pen to paper there come words, mere human words; nonetheless, from the heart there spring desires that without deliberation turn into prayer. My writings are at one and the same time my own reflections with myself and prayers to God."

We may conclude, then, that what Rafael was silently aware of in his heart, he communicated resonantly in his writings. He himself was to say:

> To speak about God and about what God achieves in creatures goes to make what really interests me in this present life. If it is not a case of speaking about God, I prefer to be silent. If I do not speak to you about God and the Virgin, what would you like me to speak to you about? I know about nothing else, and care about nothing else.

And he does it all with an elegance of expression that experts in the art of good writing are not slow to recognize. But despite the brilliance of his style, Rafael finds it difficult to put his thoughts and interior experience into words: "At times I put

aside the pen that does not say what I want to, because it neither
knows how nor is able. . . Would that I could convey with the
poor words I put into my copybook some idea of the truths that
one comes to realize only when one is silent and at *prayer*." Oc-
casionally in his writings Rafael reveals the motives behind his
writings:

> I do not presume to write in order to be read . . . I write for
> two reasons. One, because I am convinced that writing and
> treating of the things of God is very profitable for my soul
> . . . and reason two, I have the time at my disposal, and so it
> seems to me to be a way of using it for God's greater glory.

Still, besides these reasons expressly divulged by Rafael,
there are times when he writes in order to help others, telling
them how he thinks about God, how he speaks about him, while
at the same time presenting them with the heights of Christian
spirituality. Among such writings as these are found, for example,
the booklet *At the Foot of the Crucifix*, dedicated to his brother
Leopold, and the twelve "spiritual" letters written to his uncle
and aunt, the Duke and Duchess of Maqueda, from Oviedo once
his second entering of the monastery in January 1936 had been
decided. These letters are particularly worth mentioning because
Rafael wrote them with the explicit desire that once read they
be destroyed. He makes this request very clearly and strongly:
"Your letters will be read, answered and torn up. Do the same
with mine; it is on this understanding that I write to you." It
would seem that this desire that these letters should disappear,
a desire made clear even before they were written, makes them
all the more valuable, with all their spontaneity and sincerity, as
a means of knowing the soul of Rafael to the fullest extent.[1]

Lastly, Rafael sometimes wrote under obedience; for instance,
his booklet *God and My Soul* was written at the orders of his confessor, in special circumstances to be dealt with in due course.
Rafael's writings, written for different motives and about different matters, were published to some extent in the book that his

---

1. Providentially, Rafael's uncle and aunt kept these letters, which because
of their matter and form, and above all because of the good they did, particularly to his aunt Maria, can be regarded as the most significant of all his letters.

uncle, the Duke of Maqueda, wrote entitled *A Secret of La Trappe (Brother Rafael)*. Later, Rafael's mother made a compilation of her son's writings and put together the book *Writings and Biographical Details about Brother Mary Rafael Arnáiz Barón, Trappist Monk*, a book that attained its third edition before her death. Later still Rafael's writings were published under the title of *Life and Writings of Brother Mary Rafael Arnáiz Barón, Trappist Monk*, a book that in its tenth edition was made still more valuable by the addition of twelve unedited letters.

At the beginning of the Process for Rafael's beatification, a careful compilation had to be made of all his writings. Here is the list that appears in the document from the Sacred Congregation for the Causes of Saints concerning his Process, and entitled *Statement concerning the writings: Index of the Writings of the Servant of God*:

- 12 cards written to his parents and siblings
- 39 letters written to the same persons and to his grandmother, Fernanda
- 40 letters to his uncle and aunt, the Duke and Duchess of Maqueda
- 22 letters to the monks of San Isidoro de Dueñas
- 10 holy pictures inscribed and addressed to members of his family and to monks of his monastery
- A poem and some spiritual verses
- Various booklets:
  Impressions of La Trappe[2]
  The Trappist's Apologia
  Meditations of a Trappist
  At the Foot of the Crucifix or My Copybook
  God and My Soul
- Other miscellaneous original pieces

Until 1988 all Rafael's writings then available were not fully published. Discretion dictated that many details be kept under

---

2. Rafael always used *La Trapa* when mentioning his monastery, which belongs to the Order of the Cistercians of the Strict Observance. This use is retained in this book. [This translation uses the French "La Trappe" which is customary in English.—Ed.]

wraps, since they were about intimate family matters, and their disclosure could have been unwelcome to those involved. After the death at the Convent of the Incarnation (Discalced Carmelites), at Avila, of Sister Mary Clement of the Transverberation, the former Duchess of Maqueda, the aunt to whom Rafael wrote so often, it was possible, thanks to the permission of her family, to publish at long last the *Complete Works*. Nonetheless, when working on his spiritual biography earlier on, all of Rafael's writings were put at my disposal. It has seemed preferable to base this work directly on them, while filling out the biographical references with the already mentioned writings of his uncle and of his mother, and the *Statement about the Introduction of his Cause*, which among other things contains the declarations made by the witnesses at the Ordinary Process of Palencia and at the Process of Inquiry at Oviedo, with a view to the beatification of Brother Rafael, and of the judgement given by the two theologians chosen by Rome to act as censors of his writings.[3]

Finally, it must be admitted that this biography was not written for publication, but came about for reasons of study. This gives it scientific objectivity, since all that is mentioned in it is based on more than nine hundred references to Rafael's writings and to the other documentation already mentioned.[4] Suggestions from friends that it be published have been accepted, and it is done as a service to Brother Rafael's Cause, and in the hope of pleasing and helping many who are sincerely interested in getting to know him more and more, because they find that he provides both light and strength for their own personal journey to God.

3. Shortly after the publication of the *Complete Works* of Brother Rafael, some previously unknown (and consequently unedited) pieces came to light: six letters that Rafael wrote to Don Merino del Hierro, which were passed on with permission for their publication. The first five date from between August 15 and September 29, 1934. The sixth and last is dated January 3, 1936. Both their style and content tally with Rafael's other writings of that time, although certain details in them make more evident than ever some already known characteristics of Rafael. These previously unedited letters find their place in the latest edition of the *Complete Works*.

4. In order to make it easier for the reader, most mention of particular sources used has been omitted.

I

AMONG HIS OWN

Birth and family background

On April 9, 1911, at half-past eight in the evening of Palm Sunday, in the city of Burgos, Rafael Arnáiz Barón was born, the first child of a truly Catholic marriage. From the very first moment, his birth was regarded by his parents, Rafael and Maria Mercedes, as a divine blessing.

The family was well-to-do, for not only was Rafael's father a forestry engineer, but the family owned a few estates as well. It all added up to a family fortune quite sufficient to provide amply for the needs and education of the four children born of the marriage.

As regards the faith, Rafael's parents (particularly his mother) were practicing and fervent Catholics.They were honorable people of moral integrity, careful about the education of their children, considerate and fair with their servants and employees. It was in this Christian environment that Rafael lived until he entered the third level college at Madrid, and where not only his vocation to La Trappe but that of his brother Luis Fernando to the Carthusians, and that of his sister Mercedes, who entered among the Ursulines of Jesus, were fostered. The great love these parents had for their children did not prevent them from generously giving them to God in the religious state. Letters from both Rafael's father and mother leave no doubt as to their dispositions when faced with their son's decision to become a monk, dispositions full of human feelings and Christian spirit at one and the same time.

In a letter of January 10, 1934, Rafael's father wrote to the Reverend Abbot of the monastery of San Isidoro de Dueñas as follows:

Reverend Father, my son Rafael has told us of his decision to
enter the Order to which your monastery belongs, and . . . he
has asked us for our permission and consent. Although . . .
viewing the matter from an angle more earthly than that of
our son, we would have preferred that he had waited until
completing his university studies, nonetheless because, as
seems to be the case, the Lord is calling him to his service,
and has, in conformity with his divine will, so arranged things
that now is the time, we accept his plan with all reverence,
and so not only freely but most gratefully welcome the choice
that divine Providence has made of one of our children; since
God gave him to us, we are ready to give him back to Him.[1]

On January 11, Doña Mercedes expressed her reaction when
writing to her own mother, Rafael's grandmother, about his decision to become a monk:

Mother mine, on the eighth of the month my son told us of
his desire and decision to go to La Trappe . . . As becomes
a Christian, I do not rebel; I welcome and obey and give to
God the treasure so dear that he was pleased to lend me for
twenty-two years . . . We have given him full permission,
without any reservation, as God so demands, and he is going
. . . His father himself will take him to the door of the monastery . . . We believe that he should answer his call as soon
as possible. When God calls, one should answer immediately,
even if it means terrible wrenching, for delay could squander
such a clear and holy vocation . . . While his going pains me
intensely, I experience at the same time extraordinary joy at
seeing myself chosen without any deserving as the mother of
such a son . . . I dread being ungrateful to the One who has
given me so much.

1. Even more Christian was the reaction of Rafael's father when Rafael
made known his decision to enter the monastery for the second time. "When
I told him," writes Rafael, "the first thing he said was that he had made a complete donation into God's hands . . . , that the sacrifice he had made in handing
me over to God he was only too pleased to repeat, for he wanted only one thing
. . . that I should become a saint so as to be able to sanctify him . . . and that,
far from any pain or displeasure, the fact that the Lord called me so insistently,
and that he himself sees my vocation to be so sure, fills him with immense joy
and very great gratitude to God."

The behavior of Rafael's parents contributes to a better understanding of Rafael's great esteem for them when he later said, "I have just the kind of parents that I could not deserve," and he felt greatly encouraged by their generosity: "On seeing such a magnificent display of my parents' magnanimity and the glory that they were giving to God during those days, I forgot my own pains and sufferings. How could what I was doing compare with the sublime unselfishness of my parents? What magnanimity!"

Childhood and schooldays

Rafael's childhood passed quietly. From his earliest days he showed himself understanding, intelligent, easy to educate. His parents had no difficulty whatever in bringing up one so docile, with such an in-built instinct for good. Even when very small he showed his compassion and love for others. In the Process before beatification, it is reported that when one of Rafael's siblings was thirsty and asked the maid for a glass of water, he used to say, "Get up yourself, and don't bother the girl." Such compassion is all the more commendable in one so young. And the fact is that from a very early age he was moved with compassion for the hurts of others, and he avoided as far as possible being a nuisance to those about him.

At the age of eight and a half, on October 25, 1919, he received Holy Communion for the first time, in the church of the monastery of the Visitandine Sisters at Burgos. In October 1920 he entered the school of La Merced that the Jesuits had in that city, and he was exceptional for his diligence and good conduct. But all too soon he had to stay away from classes because of sickness. Although Rafael had not had any health troubles before this, on December 1 of that year he became sick owing to what was diagnosed as bacterial fever. Prevented from receiving Communion at school on Sundays when the Sodality of Mary Immaculate did so, he requested the college rector, Father Oraa, S.J., who often visited him, to bring Communion to him at home; the Father agreed to do so, and Rafael was able to receive Holy Communion every Sunday thereafter, a custom he maintained for the rest of his life.

Having moved to Madrid for the sake of better medical attention, he sent two postcards from there to his father. These, from April 1921, are the earliest samples of his writings now available, but they are so brief that they tell us almost nothing about him. Still, he tells his father that he is sending him a card painted by himself, which goes to show that he already took an interest in painting.[2]

On May 4, 1921, the pleurisy that had been dormant months before made its appearance in a rather serious way. He bore the corresponding sufferings with great patience, thus preparing himself to some extent for all the suffering that would come to him during his life, and would draw from his pen beautiful writing about the Cross. Similarly at this time there occurred an event that could well have made a positive contribution to the Marian spirituality already evident in his early youth. Once Rafael recovered from his illness, he was brought by his father to Zaragoza to offer him to the Virgin of Pilar, while giving thanks for his cure. In October of that year, Rafael returned to school, and continued his studies without further interruption.

In 1922, Rafael's father was moved to Oviedo. There Rafael and his brothers Luis Fernando and Leopoldo became day boys at the Jesuit College of San Ignacio in that city. There Rafael went ahead with his secondary education from the beginning of the school year 1923. Of this period of his life there is sound testimony that makes accessible further information about his character, about the kind of person that was being formed in him. It is the written testimony of the Prefect of the college, Father Pascual Arroyo:

> Rafael Arnáiz Barón . . . an intelligent child; his school reports witness to his diligence, and his remarkable ability at mathematics; he was not quite so remarkable at written composition, just where he was later to excel so much . . . From the very first he charmed the whole school, and was the very center and source of the gladness he radiated to his companions . . . as with genial originality and gently mocking tone, he drew to himself irresistibly all who met him. Earnest and exact about his duties, he studied hard, and reports about his studies and his conduct were always above the ordinary. Owing to his in-

2. Another childhood piece which has been preserved is a letter to the Magi that he wrote in French, from Burgos on January 2, 1922.

tense and constant piety, he was one of the committee in charge
of the Solidarity of Saint Stanislaus . . . Rafael, then, can be
described as an intelligent and cheerful child, mischievous at
games, serious at his studies, profoundly pious.

Already in Rafael's school days can be seen the beginnings of
characteristics that would later become so evident in his personality: the cheerfulness and sociability that his smile expressed even
in moments of suffering: his controlled humor, and, to balance it,
his earnestness in the fulfillment of duty; and all of it immersed
in the strong piety of personal relationship with God. Well-set in
personality and demeanor, there was nothing but normality in his
behavior; he was just like any other youngster of his age, whom all
found pleasant, while, at the same time, owing to his seriousness
and the religious content of his conversation, his schoolfellows
were already inclined to think he would become a religious.

Rafael's artistic temperament

In 1926, while continuing with his classes at school, at his
own request and with a view to his future study of architecture
he began attending classes in drawing and painting with Eugenio
Tamayo, the landscape-painter. Already from the age of thirteen,
Rafael had been attending classes in drawing, and he used to
spend all his free time at it, which explains why his home gradually filled up with sketches and colored drawings.

Love for pictorial art was always the most notable aspect of
Rafael's temperament; he saw everything through the prism of
color and form. He was gifted and very original; landscapes were
his favorite subject. It could well be that God used this preference
of his, this tendency, as a means to draw Rafael all the more to himself. Drawing, painting, expressing on canvas or card the creativity
of his artistic soul, welcoming every least suggestion of true art
was Rafael's delight, since his capacity for imagery was colossal.
This is abundantly evident in the 195 paintings and drawings of
his on exhibit in his monastery, San Isidoro de Dueñas.

His pictorial powers both in concept and in actual comple-
tion were considerable, and he was far from fussy. His teacher
says of him:

He was magnificent in the art of decoration, and had done some truly outstanding pieces . . . both in oils and in watercolor he worked to large design and without fussiness; he needed only a few highly descriptive brush strokes to bring it off; he knew how to give strength and setting to all he did. He had a very exact sense of color, and in some of his pictures he was able to achieve the most difficult tints. One peculiarity was that when Rafael did landscapes, he preferred to completely exclude from them any sign of people; none of his works contain a single human figure that could take or distract from the luminosity of the whole.[3]

This psychological trait in the artistic mode of Rafael, mentioned by his teacher, could be interpreted as a sign of misanthropy, but would seem rather to come from what was idealistic and austere in his temperament. Intensely interested in the objective that he was aiming at with pencil or paintbrush, he regarded the addition of some human figure or other as meaningless, and he used to avoid it completely; possibly he did so without noticing. As a result, the beauty of his objective appears whole and spotless in his paintings. Rafael was a person of genuine good taste. This personality trait that emerges in his art helps us better understand his decision to enter the Trappists, with all that it meant to him in its thoroughness and concentration on one single objective—*God*; he himself would prove it in his well-known *God alone* principle.

Rafael's artistic temperament did not express itself in painting only. Fluent with pencil or paintbrush or charcoal, he was also musical by nature, and played the violin, the guitar and the piano without any musical instruction, being as well able to improvise a piece of music as he was to depict some image or landscape. In addition, although without advertising it, Rafael was a poet. Unable to confine himself to meter, he did not go in for versification, but to the ease with which he wrote was added,

3. In the display of Rafael's works at the monastery of San Isidro de Dueñas, one can see a selection of his paintings, a total of 195 pictures and sketches. When there is adequate space, they will be put on display in their entirety, together with personal objects he used.

even if unsought, a deep sense of rhyme, as is perceptible in some of his prose.[4]

The period of Rafael's life when classes in drawing and painting coincided with the final years of his secondary education is further attested to by his teacher, Eugenio Tamayo, who provides plenty of detail and further information about some aspects of Rafael's meditative personality at the time that includes his first stirrings of desire for an ascetic, as yet undefined, life. Tamayo writes:

> I always remember how he used to stand silent, facing the easel for hours in my studio . . . even then I could notice something in him that drew me irresistibly . . . and as the years passed . . . I came to understand that one so special was not destined for the business of ordinary life. There was in him what drove him to ever greater heights, and before long he shared with me his intimate secrets. I was the first to hear from his own lips of his longing for an ascetic and silent life, not yet defined . . . the very life he embraced years later in that monastery of La Trappe.

It was at this time also that Rafael's artistic talent enabled him to cooperate with his mother in the theatrical productions that she helped organize for charitable and cultural purposes. On such occasions, he behaved like any normal young man, was sociable, cheerful, amused and amusing, without hurting anyone's feelings; an aficionado of good music, of artistic dancing, of poetry. He helped his mother in the preparation of the stage, which he decorated with very good taste; he also gave rehearsals for the actors, even if he himself had no desire whatever to make a public appearance on the stage, showing already that longing for hiddenness that would later lead him to the hidden life of La Trappe.

Rafael's first relations with and impressions of La Trappe

In 1929 Rafael completed his secondary education; he had just reached the age of eighteen. As a reward for completing his

4. The music of verse is clearly audible in some of the paragraphs of his *At the Foot of the Crucifix/My Copybook.*

studies and as a rest from his school tasks, his parents sent him to an estate in Avila belonging to his uncle and aunt, the Duke and Duchess of Maqueda, relatives on his mother's side, who from this time on would regard him as another of their children. Rafael's affection for and attachment to them is obvious from the fact that he wrote more letters to them than to anyone else, among which letters are the twelve "spiritual" ones he wrote to them after his first departure from the monastery, letters that, as indicated in the Introduction, are very pertinent for the story of his soul.

The spiritual friendship that now began between Rafael and his uncle and aunt came to have such depth and to be of such benefit to him that, writing to his parents from Madrid, he was to say that going to Avila was for him fully half his life. In fact, the development of Rafael's vocation to monastic life was conditioned by his relationship with his uncle and aunt. The Duke of Maqueda was described as "very Trappist," and Rafael shared his uncle's ideas to the full.

Having completed his secondary education, Rafael now began to prepare in earnest to enter the School of Architecture. Architecture, which suited his talents so well, was his great dream. After taking a degree at the University of Oviedo on April 15, 1930, he entered the College of Architecture in Madrid on April 26 of that year.[5] Once on vacation, he went to the house of his uncle and aunt at Pedrosillo (Avila) to spend some months there, where he did some paintings of Saint Ferdinand and Saint Paul for the stained-glass windows of the chapel, and he availed himself of the opportunity to go on an excursion through the different provinces of Castille, finding Salamanca most impressive. From this stay at Avila comes Rafael's first letter as an adult, one written to his father on June 23, 1930, a very pleasant piece, full of good humor. It was at this time that his Uncle Leopoldo got him to read the biography of Brother Gabriel, a Trappist Lay Brother of the monastery of Chambarand in France. Rafael read it with devout interest, and it kindled in him the desire to visit some monastery of the same order.

---

5. Rafael's natural abilities in drawing and painting facilitated his admission into the College, which was generally quite difficult to obtain.

He did not have long to wait, for following his uncle's advice, on September 21 that year Rafael paid his first visit to the Cistercian monastery of San Isidoro de Dueñas. This event was to prove decisive in the orientation and development of his life. His artistic soul was dazzled by the beauty of the chant and of the liturgy, and by the austere and silent air of spirituality in the place. In a letter to his uncle, Rafael wrote:

> The impressions I received in that holy monastery cannot be expressed or, at least, I cannot explain them, God alone knows them . . . I do not know how to explain what I mean, for when one's feelings are somewhat subtle or one experiences something supernatural, the effort to put it into words results in something silly, since it seems to me that, if one is to talk in certain ways about God, our human language is so very poor that it distorts or, at very least, is unable to convey the true meaning . . . Anyhow, I shall tell you what I did and what I saw . . . There came a moment when I began to notice and feel deep personal shame. When, on going into the church to greet the Lord, I saw the monks singing in choir, saw that altar with that statue of the Virgin, saw the reverence the monks had in church, and, above all, when I heard the Salve . . . dear Uncle Poldy, God alone knows what I felt . . . I did not know how to pray.

His experience was so engrossing that to his uncle he could write, "That day I remembered nothing, I remembered no one." Still, notwithstanding such a powerful experience, and the desire to return to the monastery and spend at least eight days there, and his wanting to drop his baggage once he reached the station, and return to the monastery, it is not altogether evident that Rafael had decided just then to become a monk. He tells his uncle in the letter:

> And you must not think that on seeing and admiring the monks, I envied them. No, because you have taught me something very important, and I have heard you mention it often: that people go to God by many paths and in very different ways; some fly, some walk, and others, the majority, just muddle through; and since God would have it so, so do I.

Nonetheless, in that same letter Rafael makes clear his willingness to enter La Trappe at some future date when he mentions answering, "If God wants it," to a monk who told him that not then, but later, once he had completed his training, he would be needed in the monastery. In fact, Rafael was so impressed, so moved, and so much enjoyed his visit to the monastery, that he would never forget the experience that made him reflect so much; he would recall it later, even as a monk:

> When that young man from the outside world saw what he saw, his soul was changed, and possibly the Lord God of Trappists used this outer impression on his senses to make him reflect. And the young man did reflect . . . God used all that was external in order to reach with his divine light that youth's somewhat dreamy soul.

Rafael went on reflecting, and living life as usual among his family. In February of 1931 he became an active member of Night Adoration at Oviedo, whereby he was able in some way, and in anticipation, to live the meaning of the night vigils he had experienced in the monastery, nourishing his spiritual life with nightly and solitary prayer, and growing in the spirit of adoration and praise. This he mentions as early as March 15 of that very year in a letter to his aunt: "Daily my contentment with life increases, and it gives me thousands of reasons and occasions for praising God."

On September 11, 1931, Rafael was in Madrid. From there he wrote to his drawing master, giving him an account of his exams, and telling him that he expected to leave for Avila within a few days. Even if no word of Rafael's explicitly confirms the fact that, in connection with this trip to Avila, he spent a day at his La Trappe on a second visit, it can be taken for granted that he did so, as in a letter to his uncle Leopoldo, conveying his impressions of his first visit to the monastery in September 1930, he tells him: "Father Armando told me not to go there during the winter: the cold would spoil it for me. So I shall go there at this time next year, when no other guests are there, and stay for at least eight days."

Moreover, it was in September 1931 that Rafael wrote his booklet, *Impressions of La Trappe*, which surely refers to this second visit to the monastery. This time Rafael's account of his impressions is more explicit than the previous one, although he still finds it difficult to give expression to his impressions. This time the impressions he describes show their greater depth when he writes:

> We must not let ourselves be led astray by our outward senses, which are usually deceptive . . . Far above all the little details that impress the visitor there is a "something," an "I know not what," impossible to put into words, and which, if faith is lacking, can never be understood . . . So that at La Trappe there happens, as the common saying puts it, "All look, but only a few are able to see" . . . An artist or a person of high sensibility is affected by La Trappe and the lifestyle of its monks, just as by a painting or a sonata . . . But a believing Christian experiences something more than that . . . experiences God in a very clear way . . . leaves the place strengthened in faith and, if the Lord gives the grace, leaves knowing himself a little better . . . and there, alone with God and with one's conscience, one's way of thinking, one's way of feeling, and, what is most important, one's way of behaving in one's ordinary life changes.

During this second visit to the monastery, Rafael looked and really saw beyond the aesthetic and musical beauty that La Trappe presented to him. He discovered that a Trappist lives in God and for God. "God is the only reason in the world for existing." His jovial and cheerful mind was able to find the deep meaning of monastic silence: that far from being empty, it is transformed into prayer:

> People will tell you that silence in a monastery is something sad, a difficult point of the Rule . . . Nothing could be more mistaken than that idea . . . Silence in La Trappe is the most cheerful jargon imaginable . . . Indeed, if God enabled us to read hearts, we would see that from a glum-looking Trappist who passes his life in silence, there flows in steady streams a gloriously jubilant song to his Creator, a song full of love for and joy in his God, the loving Father who cares for and comforts him . . . Trappists converse with God in silence.
>
> This conversing with God in prayer leads Rafael to speak of the prayer of praise and supplication of the monks in choir at liturgical prayer; and of the less formal prayer of the Lay Brothers, that in his opinion deserves all the esteem and has

all the efficacy that he describes in terms reminiscent of Saint John of the Cross: "This humble worship that surely is more pleasing to God than many deeds that the world calls charity . . . How much greater in God's eyes is a heartfelt 'Hail Mary' than even the greatest thing done without wholehearted love for God."[6]

The totality of his impressions of La Trappe reveals a Rafael who has deepened his understanding of the monastic calling by discovering the meaning of the principal values that go to make it. Does he already feel that he shares them? It would seem so, since he already had a bent for intimate union with God and for silent converse before the Tabernacle—a rather contemplative disposition. It is odd that all through his account, Rafael refers to Saint Bernard as "our Father Saint Bernard." Yes, there are grounds for holding that by this time the Cistercian spirit was penetrating his soul.

In Rafael's diary for 1932 can be seen the dates and results of his exams. Once these were over, and after a short stay at Pedro-sillo, he arrived at three o'clock in the afternoon of June 17 at the monastery of San Isidoro to make a retreat lasting until June 26 inclusive. It helped to strengthen his vocation. And yet, Rafael, who keeps noting his daily doings, and does mention a variety of activities on the other days, confines himself on June 19 to remarking, "I have become convinced of many things."

---

6. What Saint John of the Cross wrote was, "As long as a soul has not reached this state of union with God, it is becoming for it to practice love, both in the active and in the contemplative life. But once it has reached this state it is not becoming for it to busy itself in other exterior doings and practices that could in any way hinder it from attending to loving in God, even if they are of great service to God, because a little wholehearted love is more precious in the sight of God and of the soul, and of more help to the Church, although it may seem to effect nothing, than all those other deeds combined" (*Canticle* 8, Song 28,2).

II

A NEW STAGE

Rafael in Madrid: student and soldier

After leaving home, on September 17, 1932, Rafael established himself for a time at Madrid for the sake of his studies. He stayed there as a student until called up for active military service that lasted from January 25, 1933, until July 26, 1933. This meant interrupting his studies, which he would attempt to make up for in the academic year that followed by registering for quite a number of subjects, as he mentions in a letter of October 21, 1933, to his parents.

There are some letters of his in which Rafael refers to his stay in Madrid, letters that give information about his exterior activities, his state of mind and his dispositions. He displays a great sense of humor in a letter to his brother Fernando, and also his seriousness by his persistent study and his handling of intimate family business on behalf of his father or his uncle.

The tight daily schedule he kept to during his residence at the Spanish capital has survived. His day began with Mass each morning at 6:30, and ended when he went to bed at 12 midnight. Despite the intensity of his study at this period, he preferred to take time from his sleep in order to go to Mass, because he considered it the best thing to do even for the sake of his studies:

> Before now I had the good habit of going to Communion every day, and I have found from experience that by starting and putting the whole day in God's hands, everything turns out so much better; one's studies make greater progress, and were it not for the Boss, who helps me so much, I would be completely useless; and further, I must render an account of all my actions, good or bad, to Someone.

In addition to Mass, his timetable mentions a daily "visit to the Boss" from half-past eight to nine each night, and that he used to pray the Rosary before going to bed. The page on which his timetable is written is crossed by a large inscription in red that reads, "All for Jesus." It seems evident that Rafael's interior life at this period so grew and ripened that it led him to decide definitively to become a monk. In his case, a monastic vocation clearly proves to be the result of the whole spiritual process that preceded his entry to the monastery.

Nonetheless, while completely committed to Christian living and very intense in his spiritual life, Rafael has not lost his naturalness and good humor. He well knows how to join the natural and supernatural, as is demonstrated by his description of the occasion when, after praying the Rosary, he danced a jota (a lively Spanish dance for two) and play-acted a bit of *Don Juan* in the corridor of his digs. This is how he tells the story to his brother, Fernando:

> After praying the Rosary, we went into the corridor and danced a jota, then did a bit of *Don Juan*, and while I, wearing a red coverlet and with a tiny paintbrush in my hat, was addressing Doña Ines with, "Isn't it true, Angel of Love" etc., we heard some applause from the patio, coming from the landlady and all her maids . . . not knowing what to do with the coverlet, we had to continue . . . So, the very last thing you would have thought your brother was up to . . . it was *Don Juan* . . . but it could not be helped . . . I had to do something to justify wearing that coverlet and having that tiny paintbrush in the ribbon of my hat.

Rafael's days as a student in Madrid were full at one and the same time with much natural merriment and with an intense spiritual life. The friends and fellow students who had most to do with him during all of this period made the following statements during the Church Process:

> I know well he led a blameless life during that time . . . Study and piety by turns made up his life; he rose early to go to Mass, and used to make a visit [to the Blessed Sacrament] in the afternoon . . . I would like to stress that the way he expressed his piety, far from moving his young friends to think less of

him, as so often happens, and even to feel false pity for him as if he were just another weak and sickly fellow, earned him the deep respect and profound admiration of all of them, so worthy, proper and courageous was the conduct of this brave and jovial young man, endowed with all that makes for success in this life . . . He was a very quiet person who wished to achieve everything through prayer and love for his fellows; he was not of the quarreling kind. I do not recall going to the cinema with him except on one occasion, to a cinema where a documentary on a French Trappist monastery was shown. Every Sunday he used to go to a theater where Sunday concerts took place, more for the sake of something artistic than for the sake of the show . . . The extraordinary merit of his life at this time deserves commendation: there he was, free to do whatever he liked, with plenty of money, in the midst of young and frivolous companions, at the very center of noisy and merry Madrid.

And during his stay in Madrid, Rafael did not always find it easy to keep his behavior blameless; he really did have to exert himself to live up to his Christian principles. An event reported by his friend, Juan Vallaure, who was present when it happened, manifests Rafael's courage at this time when, thanks to his fortitude and presence of mind, he not only kept within limits and without shameful surrender, but was able to resist and reject in good time the suggestions and provocations of a young woman who shamelessly tried to seduce him. In the official Process, Juan tells us:

> With regard to his strength of will in restraining the flesh, I can witness to a most potent peril over which he certainly prevailed, although he himself was never fully satisfied with his conduct on that occasion. A somewhat liberated young lady stayed at our digs for almost two months. Both of us were friendly and used to flirt with her, but she took a far-from-shy liking to Rafael. One night we spent a few hours with her at an amusement arcade. When we returned to our digs, she, lightly dressed, tried to persuade him to go to bed with her; he refused absolutely. She even made her way into Rafael's bedroom, where I also slept, and lay on the bed where he already was, but could not get Rafael to yield to her unchaste suggestions. Excuse me for mentioning that Rafael had experienced

a fierce temptation of the flesh, and in order to overcome himself he had, as he told me the following day, to leave his bed
and lie on the floor . . . That it could happen at all was due to
the fact that the landing that served both her room and ours
made it quite feasible, since no one else in the house, neither
the landlady nor the servants, would have noticed a thing.[1]

With regard to the period Rafael spent doing his military
service, his friends stated at the Process:

He fulfilled his military service in Madrid, in the Engineers
. . . among his companions he dedicated himself a great deal
to the apostolate, not by preaching, but by his behavior, by
his influence . . . His conduct must have been excellent, since
he was never arrested nor punished, as happens so easily to
soldiers . . . I am quite sure that military service had no unde-
sirable effects on him, for he continued his usual life of piety
and religiosity.[2]

Preparations for entering his La Trappe

On November 19, 1933, Rafael wrote an important letter that
put an end to the struggles and doubts that usually precede important decisions, heroic though they may be. With great clarity
in his ideas, conscious of his interior development, and with corresponding decisiveness, he writes to the Abbot of the monastery
of San Isidoro and asks for admission to the community there.
Sure of what, as far as he is concerned, he wants, he is open to
advice from those whose duty it is to discern his vocation, and

1. It would seem that Rafael refers to this event in his life when he writes to
his aunt about the Virgin: "Look, years before I went to La Trappe, I had a fall,
but did not slither down to the bottom thanks to the Most Holy Virgin, who mi-
raculously snatched me out from where I was. It was not that she in some way
revealed this to me; no, but once I realized how low I could have fallen, how
close I was to doing so, and the extraordinary way in which the Lord restrained
me, I grasped, I know not why, but I was convinced, I know not how, that the
Most Holy Virgin had been responsible."
2. A recent statement of his brother Fernando tells of how Rafael used to
pray the Rosary every day with some of his fellow servicemen, notwithstanding
the anti-clericalism of the Republic and the libertinism prevalent in the barracks
he occupied.

he asks the Abbot for an interview.[3] Here are a few paragraphs from his letter to the Abbot, a letter rich in content and at the same time full of candor:

> God our Lord has been at work in me to such an extent that I have decided to give myself to him with all my heart and body and soul, and in order to carry out my purpose and resolve, and counting besides on God's help, my desire is to enter the Order of Citeaux . . . Moreover, I need only add that I am not moved to make this change in my life by sadness or suffering, nor by being disillusioned or disappointed with the world . . . all that the world could give me I already have; God, in his infinite goodness, has all through my life given me far more than I deserve . . . Consequently, Reverend Father, if you admit me to your community, you can be quite sure that you will be admitting nothing other than one with a very cheerful heart and much love for God.

Whatever inevitable anxiety Rafael, who so much wanted to give himself completely to God, may have had while waiting for the reply to his request, it was soon over, for the Novice Master of the monastery replied on the 22nd of that same month. This letter brought him peace of mind, offering him the possibility of the interview he had requested of the monastery in order to discuss his vocation, and the unconditional help of the Novice Master himself.

It is clear that Rafael soon went to his La Trappe to talk to the Novice Master. He slept there on the night of November 24, and returned to Avila on the 25th, the very day he wrote to his friend Juan Vallaure, "I have received news of the grace that the Lord has just granted to me: I have been admitted to the novitiate."

Now Rafael had to begin to prepare to enter the monastery. He would have to settle all unfinished business in Madrid, and above all, as he himself expressed it, he would have "to engage in the final battle, to face my parents," which was for him a terrible moment. In doubt as to how or when he should tell them

---

3. To judge by Rafael's own writings, there is no indication that he consulted anyone before making this decision. Still, his brother Fernando asserted during the Process: "I know he asked for advice about his vocation."

of his decision, he went with his uncle to visit the Papal Nuncio, Monsignor Tedeschini, who was then at Avila, and who in fact a few years earlier, in 1929, had consecrated the abbey church of the monastery of San Isidoro. The Nuncio not only approved of Rafael's decision to become a monk, but advised him to go to Oviedo and get the permission and blessing of his parents, and so make things all the more acceptable to all concerned. Rafael himself later recorded the Nuncio's advice:

> Things have gone in the way the Nuncio recommended to me: "Vocations should be handled in a way that not only is agreeable to God, but also is gentle and courteous to one's fellow beings; that is, in a way that is the very opposite of violent behavior, something agreeable." When this is possible, as it is in my case, it should be done that way.

Rafael would reach the goal, towards which his desire for God and his impatience would have driven him at once, little by little. He was to return on Monday, December 11, to his La Trappe, for a serious consultation with his Father Master. Then he was to go to Oviedo to tell his parents of his decision. He wished them to be the first to hear of it directly from him.[4] Following the advice of his Father Master, Rafael gradually prepared himself to inform his parents of his decision. He spent Christmas with them, as the Father Master had suggested. On January 7, once the festival season was over, he let his parents know his decision, and it was agreed that he would enter the monastery on January 15, 1934.

His health before entering

D.C.P., the physician, says in his statements during the Process, that "the diabetic condition—owing to which Rafael had to leave the monastery several times, and from which he finally died—preceded the entrance of the Servant of God at La Trappe, although he took care to hide it because it would have

---

4. All the same, Rafael's parents were not the first to learn of his decision. Due to various circumstances, he mentioned it first to his aunt and uncle, to his grandmother Fernanda, and to his aunt Maria Barón.

hindered a regular and normal life in any religious Order," and that "although I gave him treatment before he went to La Trappe, he never said a word to me about his vocation; I now suspect that he did this in order to avoid my telling him that he should not enter because he was diabetic."

These statements raise questions. Did Rafael really suffer from diabetes before he entered the monastery? Did he conceal his sickness from the community that accepted him? The doctor who witnessed at the Process says that Rafael made sure to hide it. To have so behaved towards the monastery would have rendered both his novitiate and, had he reached it, his profession null and void in Canon Law. In order to clear up these questions, Father Fernando was asked about the matter. His reply was that his brother did not have diabetes before entering the monastery. Moreover, his mother stresses all through the book that she published the good health of Rafael, who had never suffered a recurrence of the sickness he had when a child. He had had good health before and during his military service, which he proved well able for, and she says that he left home for the monastery "bursting with life and health."

The medical certificate given to Rafael in view of his military service states unquestionably that "he shows no sign of sickness or of physical defect, and enjoys good health at all times." True, it dates from January 10, 1933, a year before he entered the monastery. That he was in good health during his military service, as his mother affirms, does not exclude the possibility of his having afterwards experienced some of the symptoms of diabetes during the six months before he entered.

Still, a friend of Rafael's stated expressly during the Process, "I know that Rafael became ill after entering La Trappe." In addition, it is a fact that D.C.P. was not Rafael's family doctor until the death in 1936 (during the Civil War) of Dr. Laredo, whom Rafael describes in a letter to the Father Infirmarian of the monastery as, "Dr. Laredo, my physician." Taking all this into account, is it credible that Rafael, after military service, discovered he had diabetes and hid the fact from his family and friends; and that, in order to keep the secret more safely, he consulted a physician other than the one his family then had, and in turn, hid from him his desire to become a monk?

The answer, in all honesty, would seem to be in the negative, for the following reasons:

1. Such behavior is completely at variance with the trustful relationship Rafael's letters show he had with his parents.

2. It seems odd that spending quite a while in Madrid after completing his military service, he should go to a doctor in Oviedo in order to conceal his sickness from his family.

3. In any event, his mother in Oviedo or Juan Vallaure, who shared his digs in Madrid, would have known about Rafael's medication, and still more about the particularly strict diet his ill-health demanded. Juan Vallaure, for his part, stated in the Process, "I am certain that, while I stayed on at the Callao digs, Rafael became ill, apparently with diabetes, so that he had to leave and find a cure at home." Reference has already been made to his mother's assertions about his good health.

4. Given the weariness that his ill-health caused, Rafael would have found it difficult to keep to the tight schedule in Madrid that his timetable describes. And he would not have been capable of the regular life he lived in the monastery during the four months that preceded his leaving because of sickness. Still less could he have been able to truly mention good health, as he explicitly does when he says, "During the four months of novitiate [I had] not even a bad headache: [my] health was terrific and [I] led a charmed existence."

5. Lastly, Rafael's interior disposition before entering the monastery makes it unthinkable that, had he had some sickness or other at the time, he would not have made it known to the Father Master during their earliest conversations, the very time at which he had surrendered his whole life to the will of God. Moreover, his personal honesty and sincerity were not exactly conducive to concealment in one who was totally truthful, and never went in for double-dealing nor was ever found to tell a lie, as his brother Fernando stated during the Process.

It seems, therefore, that D.C.P. is inaccurate in his statements —statements he made thirty years after the events—because he confuses Rafael's various entrances into the monastery. There can be no doubt that he gave Rafael treatment as soon as possible after his first departure, once the diabetes had already manifested itself while he was at the monastery. That Rafael told him nothing about his vocation could have been due to his dread of being misunderstood, as had so often happened to him. In any case, there is an instance when Rafael did exactly the opposite. One month before his second entrance into the monastery, and entering as an oblate, he writes: "I have told him [the doctor] how I am and what I am about to do . . . He thinks it a good idea . . . he has prescribed a very strict diet." There are reasons for thinking that here he is referring to Dr. Laredo, who was then his family doctor.

His state of mind before entering

Because of all the letters that Rafael wrote to the monastery or to members of his family during the period preceding his entering, his state of mind, his interior, is quite perceptible. His decision to become a monk is clearly the result of an interior process that has been developing within him for some time. It is, above all, a response to the call of God, with whom he wants to fill himself, and who, moving his heart through the gifts of the Spirit, makes it easy for him to respond:

> I have been thinking about it for years, and for years God has been lovingly and gently calling me. Consequently, as far as I am concerned, there is only one thing to do, that is, to go . . . When I make my examination of conscience and look within myself for a little while, it is quite clear to me that I am merely following the dictates of what my heart wants from God, longing for nothing else than to fill myself with him. The real sacrifice would be to go on being the world's prisoner, unable to praise him day and night in choir . . . For a long time now my heart has been cutting itself loose from things and coming close to God.

And Rafael is so conscious of God's action in his life that he discloses to his Father Master the fear he has of not being faithful to God's grace, and of his need of purification because of how things really are with him:

At times not knowing how to correspond makes me afraid, since my behavior has been rather mediocre; I am neither fervent nor mortified nor really in any way different from other people . . . Father, if only you could see how much useless "ballast" I have to drop before I appear before God! How little others know us! In the very midst of a devout life, so much mud clings to one!

He considers that his life ought to be a response to all God does and has done for him; an offering made out of pure love for God; this is evident from a dedication he addressed to his mother:

Mother . . . I give everything to him . . . all that I have and whatever I am worth I give to him with all good will and from the heart, and all that I now ask is that he accept it . . . Mother, you too ask this from him, and say, "Lord, my son offers you his life and his deeds, and hands himself over completely to you. Do not refuse his offering, which, although always imperfect, he makes out of pure love for you . . . Lord, accept my son: it is a mother who asks this of you." And thus both you in the outside world and I in the monastery have something to offer to God. I offer all that I am and you offer your son.

Together with this offering of his whole being to God out of love, Rafael mentions other motives for following his vocation: he goes to the monastery to make his life one of unceasing praise to God, and in order to become a saint, thereby accepting God's plan for him:

The only comfort that creatures can have is to delight in God; that is what I go to La Trappe to do. There seven times a day, as King David used to do, I shall sing songs in his honor . . . The monastery for me will mean two things: one, a corner of the world in which I can praise God unhindered day and night; and two, a purgatory on earth where I can purify myself and become a saint . . . Put that way, coolly as that . . . becoming a saint would seem a trifle presumptuous . . . I do not know how else to express it . . . Still, it is true: I do want to become a saint in God's estimation, not in that of others; the kind of sanctity that grows in silence and that God alone will know, and not even I will notice, for otherwise it would not be genuine sanctity . . . I read some lines recently that said, "Virtue in anticipation is not virtue" . . . I shall be content with whatever God wants and allows me to become; I hand over my will and my good desires to him; it is for him to do the rest.

This spirit of praise is so powerfully present in Rafael that in his writings at this time it occupies a predominant place, leaving other forms of prayer a little to one side:

If only you knew how much he loves me and how he has supported me and keeps supporting me! You would neither ask nor offer him anything. Everything would boil down to unceasing praise, to blessing and glorifying him, to the constant lilt of a glorious song of thanksgiving and gratitude . . . Praise God at every moment; there is no prayer that God is more grateful for, nor is there any other prayer that brings us closer to him; soon that will be my life . . . praising God at every moment.

Moreover, this spirit of praise corresponds to Rafael's idea of God. He has discovered him as the Absolute, as the uniquely important One, in whose light all else is to be viewed, whom one must seek and contemplate:

All such [sufferings] are child's play in comparison with the great Truth . . . the only Truth that God is . . . All that is important is to seek him and, once one has found him . . . there are neither pains nor joys, there is nothing . . . There is nothing except God, who fills everything, floods everything . . . To find him one must seek him in the cross, in self-denial and in sacrifice . . . It is then that God shows himself to us, and then indeed prevents us from seeing anything else, for he is so *absorbing* that there is then nothing except himself.

Thoughts like these make it no surprise when Rafael says: "God is my only addiction . . . God and my vocation is all that interests me." And it is God perceived particularly as the Absolute that Rafael goes to the monastery to seek, as Saint Benedict wants a postulant to do.[5] And although Rafael has made up his

5. See Rule of St. Benedict 58.7.—Ed.

mind about this above all, it does not prevent him feeling the pain that the separation from his family will bring to his relatives. This is a great trial for him. The days spent with his family before making his decision known made for the painful situations that he often mentions in his letters:

> What great demands God makes of me! He not only demands that I leave all, but before I do so for good, he demands that I do so beforehand . . . I have not yet said a word, for any trifle weakens me; some sign of affection . . . some kind action of my mother's; why, the situation becomes increasingly unbearable for me . . . I lack the energy to inflict the wound, and it is not as if I were unscathed, my wound bleeds already . . . it is not as if there were danger for my vocation; on the contrary, I am more content than ever with the path I have taken and more resolute about it all; for me God comes first, and with his help I shall be able to overcome creatures; and if afterwards the only thing I can offer is a heart covered with blood, it will be because he has wanted it that way, and he will take care to heal it for me, for it will belong completely to him . . . I have to spurn and shatter many things; but these shatterings are only for a moment . . . later the wounds are healed and God takes full possession of us; that fondness, which it seems at first that we renounce, grows and, above all, purifies itself . . . and purifies itself in God.

The nearness of the moment when he must tell his parents of his decision makes him so much afraid that he overcomes it only by great confidence in help from on high: ". . . the moment approaches, and I would be telling a lie were I to say that I do not fear it; still, at the same time, I have such great confidence in God's protection, that it enables me to go ahead and face up to it all."

In fact, Rafael is ready for all that it takes to respond to God. He realizes and accepts the demands of his monastic vocation, with all the heartfelt loneliness as well as the separation from his family that it involves, in order to draw closer to God:

> When the soul is called by God, he would have it so completely detached that he strips it even of the external comfort that creatures provide, and when the soul sees itself alone, deserted and seemingly deprived of everything . . . then, as I

understood it, is when God is closest to it, and then the voice
of God's will is most clearly audible.

Nonetheless, despite this acceptance of solitude and the detachment that it demands with regard to one's own family, Rafael,
who had experienced in a very deep way how welcome he was to
his own family and deep Christian joy in its midst, experienced
also that the separation in question means no lack of affection: "You
must not think that I am distancing myself . . . on the contrary, I
am drawing close to God . . . Consequently, I do not renounce
fondness for my family, which is so beautiful and human . . . I only
want to change it into something sublime and divine."

This situation, what with his great natural affection for his
nearest and dearest and the pain they would suffer because of his
leaving them in order to follow the call of the Lord, produces in
Rafael a state of mind that is difficult to put into words because
of conflicting emotions right up until shortly before he enters
the monastery:

> Mixed with my tears and my heart in shreds, go a gladness
> and contentment and a tranquility of mind that is hard to
> understand; in fact, what I am going through is of its nature
> rather odd . . . what goes on within me is so great . . . for not
> only is my gladness great, my pain is great, very great . . .
> but greater still is my love for God . . . ; were it otherwise, I
> could not bear it.

During these difficult, final moments of being with his family, while he experiences such conflicting emotions, God's grace
is not lacking to Rafael, who can be seen in his last two letters
before entering the monastery still experiencing and depending
on help from on high: "The most holy Virgin helps me in such
a way that I almost physically experience it . . . I have absolute
confidence in God, which has never been lacking to me and, I
hope, will never be lacking to me."

On January 15, 1934, at nine o'clock in the morning, Rafael
left home at last, with his father who brought him to the monastery by car. His mood was calmer than that of all who were
present at his departure. Some hours later his father left him at
the monastery of San Isidoro de Dueñas.

III

IN MONASTIC LIFE

A joyful experience

At last Rafael was able to live the monastic life he had so ardently desired. Fifteen days after entering the monastery, he writes about his adaptation to this new kind of life to his mother: ". . . it seems as if I had arrived only yesterday. By now I am well used to the Rule, which at first sight and from the outside seems hard, but the only hard thing is the bed . . . The rest is austere, but not inhuman nor just a little less."[1]

Time would help him to adapt more completely to monastic observance, and so a month later he tells his parents once again: ". . . by now I am getting used to everything. The body is a creature of habit, and the only remedy is to know how to control it." But this adaptation, this getting used to everything, was not achieved without struggle and suffering. Rafael himself, after he left the monastery, would tell his uncle Leopoldo:

> It is also true that at the beginning it cost me many tears, for after all I am a human being with heart and feelings, and some things are inevitable. I remember my first days as a postulant when we used to go out to the fields in single file . . . more than once in those days I would drench the lumps of earth that my hoe worked loose with huge tears the size of oranges. Soon I would pull myself together; I would recall the question that our Father Saint Bernard would ask himself: "Bernard, for what have you come?" . . . Then I would redouble my efforts at the work.

1. Still, despite assuring his mother about his austere but not hard life, thinking over his experience later Rafael would say, "I assure you that the life is hard, very hard, but it keeps God so near that one does not notice the austerity of the Rule . . . I am convinced that without a special grace a Trappist could not live."

Clearly Rafael is no stranger to ascetic effort. It means turning the whole person towards God, bringing together for this purpose all the elements that go to make a person, both body and mind:

> Blessed nature, what conflict you provoke! But wait, and with God's help I shall get the better of you and tame you; to do this I need only one thing, namely, constancy and prayer . . . and undoubtedly after a while, without my noticing it, I will need less sleep than at present; but it is going to be done! . . . Today . . . we have two hours of work or, in other words, two hours of complete silence, and I can say for sure that I become neither tired nor bored, since what I do is reflect. Put that way, it seems nonsense, for everyone reflects. But that is not the way it really is. To reflect is a difficult thing. Of course I mean worthwhile reflection, reflecting in an orderly way, benefiting by it, reflecting calmly, restraining and leading the imagination where one wants to.

Knowing well why he has come to the monastery, Rafael has to restrain also the natural impulses of his cheerfulness and good humor for the sake of the observance of silence, the silence that he deeply loves and regards as one of the holiest characteristics of the Rule of Benedict; he even goes as far as to say:

> The most beautiful thing in La Trappe is the silence . . . how gladly would I have a chat with my dear fellow monks . . . I am convinced that silence is a great help in keeping one from losing the presence of God . . . but it is a great penance, above all at certain times; for instance, some splendid day you are on the way to work in the fields; fieldwork is cheerful; well, the cheerfulness that you would like to display by jumping about and singing, you have instead to keep quiet about and offer to God in silence . . . that is very beautiful, but it takes getting used to. I told the Father Master that sometimes I would just love to shout for joy, and he replied that I should keep my energy for singing in the choir, and I do just that.[2]

---

2. Nonetheless, despite his usual self-control for the sake of observance, one who was present tells an amusing story: "One day a group of novices and oblates was heading for the fields; it was a very beautiful morning; the mild and scented atmosphere, the radiantly blue sky of Castille bright with splendid

It is in self-renunciation and surrender to God that Rafael finds the source of his joy and peace:

> How very different is the idea that people have about a Trappist monastery . . . ! How many there are who feel sorry for me, in addition to being scared by the way I now live, without even suspecting that right here, in self-renunciation and complete surrender to God, is found the only thing worth the trouble of living . . . namely, peace in God!

In fact, although living a life so much at variance with the life he had led outside, for Rafael these first months in the monastery are an experience of peace, gladness and contentment. He feels his deepest longings are completely fulfilled. He is conscious of the joy one experiences when one is what one ought to be in one's life. He makes this perfectly clear to his parents:

> Your son has found the right road . . . I am more and more convinced that God has made La Trappe for me, and me for La Trappe; obviously the only worthwhile skill in this world is to place ourselves where God has destined us to be . . . and once we have succeeded in discovering his will, to give ourselves to him wholeheartedly.

This knowledge that he is where God would have him be, and awareness that he accepts the monastic values he has embraced, explains why in almost all the letters that Rafael wrote at this time, there appears some reference to his living contentedly, gladly, joyfully. It is the most noticeable constant that makes its appearance. Everything, including externals, seems to contribute

---

sunshine; the bird-song, the peace, the calm and tranquility of conscience; it all made an exuberant gladness well up within us that we could barely contain. Our saint was unable to repress it, and picking up a little piece of hollow wheat stubble, he made a whistle out of it and produced a few sounds. The whole group laughed, and soon the oblates and a few of the novices, each with their own whistle, made the field ring with a melodious and merry tune. Authority interrupted the proceedings, and to the distress of the buskers, everything returned to silence. Our dear brother later accused himself of being responsible for the racket."

In his recent book *El Hermano Rafael: Recuerdos íntimos*, Fr. Damián Yañez gives a different version of this incident.

to his joy, which springs even from monastic poverty itself or his
having calluses on his hands:

> Here in La Trappe is where I have seen the greatest concentra-
> tion of gladness . . . And, besides, God treats us so well that
> we just cannot be sad . . . that would be to sin against him . . .
> How happy I am here in my monastery, having only a robe and
> a white cloak for all my belongings, and I can see that nothing
> more is needed to be happy . . . It is a great comfort to have
> calluses for the love of God . . . Every day I am more content
> to be a Trappist monk; that is something beyond all price.

Not even the apparent monotony of monastic life, so regu-
lated by a tight timetable, can dampen the gladness of Rafael,
who is able to find or extract novelty from what could easily
become routine. Thus, while his days slip by with all speed, he
reaches the stage of making his whole life a continuous chant to
his Creator:

> For me this life, that seems so monotonous, has so many
> charms that it does not tire me for as much as a moment;
> every hour is different, for although outwardly they are all of
> a piece, inwardly they are not . . . I have no spare time . . .
> My days fly by . . . life in La Trappe boils down to singing in
> choir and singing outside of choir, making sounds at the for-
> mer and being silent at the latter time, but the song is all one.

Thus Rafael lives his first months of monastic life, having God
alone for his goal, busy only with loving him. Although he lives
day by day quietly waiting for God to call him, he longs for the
face-to-face sight of God, whom he begs to take him from the monastery to heaven that there he may continue his song. It would
seem that for Rafael, to be a Trappist monk was already the full
culmination of his desires in this world; why, he even goes so far as
to say, ". . . now I can die content . . . now that I am a Trappist."

The illness that changed it all

Rafael, "who was too happy in La Trappe," as he would later
say, whose farewell to the outside world was something defini-
tive as far as he was concerned, could not have had the least

suspicion that God, who drew him so strongly to monastic life, had plans for him that did not include his staying permanently in the monastery. Yet, as will become evident, God's plan for him did indeed exclude just that.

At the very time that the Father Master, writing on March 5 to Rafael's mother, was telling her that "he continues in wonderfully good health, despite the raw winter weather, and is bearing up well with the fasting during Lent," and Juan Vallaure, who found Rafael "more tanned, heavier and stronger," was telling her, "you need not worry, Rafael is in perfect health, better than ever, and is altogether happy," the illness that would end his life was already hovering over him. Early in May, the first symptoms of diabetes and their accompanying burden of tiredness and weakness began to appear. By the middle of the month, Rafael was unable to do his full share of the fieldwork with his brother monks. Once his lack of energy and his paleness became noticeable, he was ordered to rest or to leave aside the task he was doing. Meanwhile, although he suffered greatly, he said nothing. It was only on June 3 that, in a letter to his uncle Leopoldo, he gave a detailed account of the course of his illness. Meanwhile, things became so serious that on May 24 Rafael's father received the following letter from the Father Master:

> My dear Sir and esteemed friend,
> Just when it was furthest from our thoughts, it has today been certified that Rafael is suffering from diabetes mellitus, which can be remedied by proper treatment and the right medication. After consultation our doctor thinks it best that you should take Rafael home with you, and there get him treatment as soon as possible. Consequently, and with regret, I beg you drive here and take him away; all pertinent advice will be given you here.

This letter put an end to the four months of peace, quiet joy and useful learning in God's service that Rafael had spent in the monastery. Just when he thought that, after his past struggles and the great sacrifices he had made, he had reached the immediate goal of his vocation, he had to return once again to the outside world. In a terrible state of physical exhaustion, pale, blind, almost at death's door, having lost fifty-three pounds in a week, but still smiling as if he was the happiest person on earth, Rafael arrived on May 26 at his parents' home from which four months earlier he had set out bursting with life and health. A little later, back in his own bed, attended and surrounded by doctors and every kind of care, he calmly, although with limitless sadness in his kind look, said "As you can see, here I am again . . . God wants it!"

The esteem of his brother monks in the monastery

The community of San Isidoro could not avoid being much affected by the loss of a novice, who, during the time he spent in the monastery, had been noted for his gentleness and kindness. Now, with great grief, the brothers beheld him almost dead with exhaustion. His appearance reflected much suffering, yet he could keep smiling with the cheerfulness and peace that come from God. Rafael's parents bear witness to this attitude of the community towards their son. In a letter of May 28, written by his mother to Father Marcelo, the Novice Master, telling him about the improvement in Rafael's health, she says, among other things:

> My husband arrived home very moved by the fond farewell all the Superiors had given to my son, and most grateful for all their proofs of affection . . . and I have every reason to bless them for their great love for my Rafael and for how well they have understood him and won his affection.

Father Marcelo, when gratefully replying to this letter, does so in a manner that shows the community's concern about and esteem for Rafael:

> The arrival of your letter has relieved the anxiety that we all shared. All keep asking me continually if I have any news for them, because all are equally interested about the health of one who constantly showed that La Trappe was where he belonged, and when your hoped-for letter arrived it filled us all with gladness.

Among other details in a long and affectionate letter written to Rafael, Father Marcelo himself tells this: "Your companions

[in the Novitiate] keep asking me constantly when you will return and encourage them by your good example, and I do not
know what to answer." There can be no doubt that Rafael's fellow monks were able to discover and appreciate the human and
supernatural richness of his personality. This was made clear
in the statements made at the introduction of his Cause. They
found him pleasant, cheerful, charming, lovable, helpful, charitable in his dealings with others, and not lacking in healthy good
humor; for, as a good community person, he really enjoyed community life, and had found "love for neighbor and charity" in
the monastery.[3]

Rafael really loved the Rule, which he observed without exceptions until he became ill, and his conduct was blameless with
regard to keeping the observances of the monastery. Above all,
during the Divine Office, which for him constituted the essence
of Trappist life, he gave the impression of being truly pleased
and content. In fact, he himself had admitted, "What I like best
is being in choir," while at the same time he edified his brother
monks by his piety.

The high esteem the community had for Rafael can be
summed up in the opinion expressed by Father Hipólito Gon-
zalez, who had taught him Latin in the monastery: "We all considered him the best novice, and we were going on supernatural
principles," which helps one to understand better what the Abbot
said to Rafael as he was leaving the monastery: "You must return;
consequently, I order you to obey the doctor as if he were the
Father Master." The Abbot, in addition to giving Rafael a part-
ing blessing and embrace, gave him also (although it was quite
unusual) the Habit he had clothed him in three months earlier. It
could be used as a shroud in the event of his death. Still, although
having it meant much to Rafael, the fact is that he never wore it
while he was at home.

---

3. With regard to Rafael's love for community life, there is a rather reveal-
ing and likeable detail: "While chatting one day with his brother, who was preparing to enter the Carthusians, the latter said to the Servant of God, 'Why do
you not become a Carthusian?' To this he replied . . . , 'I need to see faces.'"

IV

RETURN TO WHAT HAD BEEN LEFT

Reflecting on his experience

Rafael had once said that he would prefer to live for only a month in La Trappe rather than return again to the outside world, since "nothing in the world outside attracted him"; now he found himself again outside the monastery. Although the situation was distressing, he was able to accept it as God's will for him, and he applied himself to live in his present condition by striving for a cure, entrusting himself totally to the Lord's hands.

Since Rafael was unable to write to the monks himself, his mother did so in the letter of May 28 to Father Marcelo already mentioned. She gave an account of the arrival and state of the patient, and described in great detail the intense medical care bestowed on him. Thanks to this, and despite the unanimous medical opinion about the seriousness of his condition, Rafael emerged from the danger. On June 3, he was able to write his first letter to his uncle Leopoldo, even if his sight was still not good and he tired easily. In this letter, he gives his interpretation of the events he has just been through:

> What I am going through is quite straightforward; what it amounts to is that God loves me very much . . . I was happy in La Trappe, I considered myself the most fortunate of mortals; I had been able to detach myself from creatures and my only ambition was God . . . But still I had kept one thing: love for La Trappe, and Jesus, who is very possessive about the affection of his children, wanted also that I detach myself from my love for my monastery, even if only for a time.

With his distinctively affectionate personality, Rafael loved his monastery with the kind of love that includes an all too human

illusion. His heart was attached to all that the external world of
the monastery offered him, just as it was to the superiors who
had a paternal regard for him, and above all to those brothers in
religion who were very fond of him. The Lord had come to sever
the shoots that his heart was extending, the shoots that could
hinder his flight to the heights. He himself says so in a letter to
his Father Master:

> The lesson that I am learning is very useful, for my heart is
> still very attached to creatures, and God wants me to detach
> it in order to give it to him alone. Look, Father, the day I left
> the monastery, when during the Office of None I was in the
> gallery, dressed in ordinary clothes, at the very time that the
> Fathers were chanting, I shed very bitter tears when looking
> at them and seeing myself uprooted from the choir . . . I bade
> farewell to them all in my heart, being unable to embrace them
> . . . and after drying my eyes, I perceived that those tears
> would have been more pleasing to God if, instead of looking
> so much at my brothers in religion, whom I love so much, I
> had looked more at the tabernacle . . . Do you not agree? . . .
> After all, it is more sad to leave God's house than it is to sepa-
> rate oneself from one's fellows . . . but the heart obeys no or-
> ders, and mine is one that has always made me suffer . . . and
> since God wants me to mature and improve, it is evident that
> this hard trial that he sends me is something necessary . . . Of
> course, I make no effort to rid myself of those feelings, all that
> God wants me to do is to make them perfect, and with that in
> view he takes me from here to there as if I were a plaything,
> leaving shreds of my heart on all sides. Father Marcelo, how
> great God is, and how well he does it all!

In a letter to his uncle, Rafael reveals the interior disposition
with which he lives out this purification the Lord is inflicting on
him with his departure from the monastery:

> The trial I am going through is hard, very hard, but I neither
> tremble nor am I frightened, nor do I lose confidence in God.
> I see his hand all the time in all that happens and comes my
> way, and I assure you that it is very pleasant to surrender one-
> self into the hands of so good a Father.

Rafael acknowledges the absolute dominion of God over his existence, and all the more so from the moment he offered it to him. He takes it that what has happened is the result of the offering he made to the Lord, to whom he wants to remain faithful above all:

> Once one hands oneself over unreservedly to God, one must be ready for everything . . . I offered myself to him, and he accepted me. . . When I went to La Trappe, I surrendered to him all that I had and all that I possessed: my soul and my body . . . My surrender was absolute and total; it is altogether right, then, that God should now do with me whatever pleases him and seems best to him; and on my part there must be neither complaining nor rebelling . . . The trial that he demands of me is hard, but with his help I will go forward; here, there or wherever, I will go forward, unyielding. I have put the hand to the plow and I must not look back.

The trial that he has experienced and is experiencing has enabled Rafael to grow spiritually. Perceiving and accepting the purifying process to which the Lord has subjected him could not prove fruitless. He himself says so:

> the lesson has been helpful . . . Now I understand very well that extremely narrow road referred to by Saint John of the Cross . . . and why he says, "Nothing, nothing, nothing" . . . Before drawing close to God there is nothing for it but to strip oneself of *everything* and remain with *nothing* . . . What more can I give to God once I have given my vocation?

Improvement in health and thinking of returning

Nonetheless, Rafael asks the Lord to cure him that he may return to the monastery and to his brother monks. He asks for health in order to give it back once again; he wants it for no other reason. His longing to return appears very frequently in his letters at this time, from the first ones to his uncle and to his Father Master, respectively. It is the result of a certainty he has experienced interiorly, a certainty sensed more or less strongly, and that increases his longing:

This illness is of very long duration, and I have no idea when
I may be fit to return . . . I have no idea when it will happen, but God assures me that I will die a Trappist . . . I have
great confidence in God; he will certainly bring me back to the
monastery; I think of nothing else all day. . . Go on praying
for me to the most holy Virgin, our Lady, for I myself do so
that we may be able to resume my novitiate . . . after all, that
is where I belong.

That is where I belong! After a few months' experience of
living in the monastery, Rafael had said that God had made La
Trappe for him and him for La Trappe; now he arrives once more
at the same conclusion, a conclusion in apparent contradiction to
the life it is now his lot to live outside, a life he realizes is not his
at all. He says as much to the Father Master: "Father, if only you
could see how displaced I am in the world outside."

His mother sees him that way as well. She knows that Rafael
accepted God's plan for him, and she also knows that, although
he has returned home, he is still a Trappist, as he himself says
in a letter to his grandmother. No doubt, once the first intensive
care demanded by his serious condition had passed, and the improvement in his health became more and more marked, Rafael
returned to being his usual self. But his mother, even as she realized how normal his behavior was, what with his cheerful chats
with his siblings and friends, and although he had resumed his
smoking, his playing the violin, and above all his painting, she is
well aware of his "irrevocable decision to return, in a more or less
short time, to his happy life as a Trappist monk." That is where
he belongs. And his mother says so very plainly in her letters to
the Father Master: "We can see that he belongs there and that
his mind is always absent from us, from our home and from our
life . . . I read his homesickness for his La Trappe in his eyes, his
restless longing to return to it."

Thanks to a rigorous diet and the proper dosage of insulin
to control the diabetes, Rafael had so improved that he planned
a trip to La Trappe for the Abbot's feast-day, August 1, and he
thought he would like to stay there until August 3. He did just
that, and those days were a real gift of God for him; "he needed
them as much as he needed to eat." They were, so to speak, a
sign of God's closeness to him in the trial he was undergoing;

the closeness of God who knows the measure of his creature's stamina, and to whom he gives a hand when things are made difficult by the length of the trial.

Rafael's visit to the monastery seems to have strengthened his longing to return to it. This idea had so rooted itself in his mind that he mentioned it with decisive firmness and sureness:

> My vocation is increasingly more firm and sure; every day that passes, my conviction that La Trappe is where I belong keeps growing . . . my trust in God is so great that *I am certain* that I will return . . . Each should be left go their several ways . . . mine is perfectly clear . . . And if now, when my complete cure is so near, I were to turn back, it would be unpardonable of me . . . Such a possibility does not enter my head.

He simply has to return because he is and continues to be a Trappist, and for him to be a Trappist means:

> not wanting anything except what God wants; that he [God] be his one and only occupation, his one and only desire, his one and only love and occupation . . . That he be full of the Spirit of God and that all the activities of his life be directed exclusively to him, for his greater glory and in his name.

And Rafael knows that this is possible for him only in the monastery, where God was his only dream. It is precisely from this fact that his very ardent desire to return to it proceeds. "The Trappist that I have within me," Rafael says, "emerges almost always without my wanting him to." And he is not always understood by many, who cannot fathom his decision to return to the monastery: "Many either admire me or take me for a madman once they come to know of my firm decision to return to La Trappe. But God, who knows everything, is well able to see that neither reaction is justified."

Why, at times Rafael meets with misunderstanding even more directly from someone in whom he has confided:

> The other day I met a one-time schoolfellow of mine, a very good lad and very good Christian; we began, as was to be expected, by talking about La Trappe; so I told him that, once

I had fully recovered, I would once again make my way there, to my monastery . . . Well, without his wishing to disturb me, far from him any such thing, he called me selfish, half-suicidal, and also lousy.

The Trappist's Apologia

It is in the context of this misunderstanding by many that Rafael decides to write *The Trappist's Apologia*, begun on September 19, 1934. Although he gives his reasons for writing right at the start, it seems right to think that he is truly interested as well in defending his own vocation, the monastic life he loves so much, which is such a contradiction to the outside world in which it is his lot in life to live. There can be no doubt that the ideas he here expounds are conditioned by his experience of the monastic life he had lived for some time. And indeed, Rafael, who "helped by God's enlightenment would give himself to reflection and meditation there at La Trappe," changed a lot during his four months in the novitiate, when God let him see things he had not seen before. Now in some of his writings he shows himself well-acquainted with the spiritual life and with the discernment of spirits, but in his own case above all what stands out is his living by faith in God as the Absolute. He certainly had this sense of God before he entered the monastery, but now he experiences it in a very vivid way; he is conscious of his belonging to God and of being inundated by God: "First God, always God and only God . . . He is all and fills all . . . God inundates me . . . I belong to God, God is my goal and is the only one able to fill me completely. . . All else I have no need of; it is completely unnecessary for me."

This idea of God, strongly sensed as uniquely necessary, does undoubtedly color Rafael's idea of life and of the world. It is an idea of Providence tending to eternity. He views everything "through the prism of God"; he cannot view it otherwise nor does he want to. He himself will tell us, "I am 'Trappist,' and as 'Trappist' I sense, see and speak." Given this view of life and of things, it is easier to grasp his way of reflecting on the occupations and preoccupations of this present life, its brevity, one's body and the riches that are so ephemeral and paltry, as viewed in this

Apologia. "What real importance for us has what is here below?" Rafael had already asked. "Having spent some time in a Trappist monastery where everything, absolutely everything is focused on the greater glory of God," he feels hurt that the outside world lives in a manner so hostile to the things of God. As regards the outside world, Rafael adopts differing viewpoints, some of them very pessimistic, which seemingly correspond to the different meanings that the "world" has in the Bible.

He clearly considers it an amalgam of the evil spirit's forces that set themselves in opposition to the kingdom of God. Viewed this way, Rafael is ready to oppose it with his whole being:

> The incompatibility of the love of God with the spirit of the world is, then, all too evident . . . for I clearly see that the world is God's enemy, and with God's enemy no agreement can be reached no matter how small, no quarter given . . . I shall fight you with fist and foot . . . You are God's enemy, and therefore you are mine as well.

And yet when Rafael decided to go to La Trappe he did not do so because he feared the outside world. He himself asserts that "if a monk withdraws to the cloister, it is in order to praise God with greater freedom." On this point he accepts as true the rather pessimistic description of the outside world given by Father Faber in his book *The Creator and the Creature* when describing how a contemplative ought to view it. However, Rafael disagrees with him for describing it in such a gloomy way, where everything is evil, everything is sin, everything is danger, all is dreary; Rafael's experience was very different. For him the world, understood as the cosmos, is a manifestation of God. He thinks that if nature amazes and thrills us, it is because its Author is present. In point of fact, in his writings at this time, Rafael shows himself a real contemplative, able to find God in everything:

> It is joy and blessing to see the goodness of God reflected in creatures . . . If a landscape moves me, it is because I see God in it, and the colors, the winds, and the sun are his creatures . . . So, let us praise him . . . In creatures too, be they human or irrational, I see God, and praise him for the greatness of souls, and entreat him for the wretchedness of bodies . . . I

see God also in the events of life, and I associate everything with him . . . I see that creation is beautiful, I rejoice with the souls of those who love God . . . Life is not sad when one possesses God . . . The sun is bright, I like the flowers, the birds, the children. *Everything* is a reason for praising the Creator: the stars, the night and the light-filled fields; and in a Trappist monastery one enjoys all that because it all leads one to God . . . Whenever we see a creature that delights us . . . we should see God in it.

Lastly, with regard to the world of people, of humankind, Rafael's attitude is brotherly, full of kindness and fellowship. He says so very clearly:

My leaving La Trappe has enabled me to view my fellow humans in a way that I did not know of previously; that is to say, viewing people as my fellow beings who do not know the Father . . . My thinking is more Trappist, and a Trappist judges kindly . . . It hurts . . . to see people are so blind . . . I do not consider people bad; I love them all, and I suffer on seeing my fellow humans suffer . . . The forgetfulness of creatures with regard to their Creator . . . makes me suffer . . . The sight of people's ingratitude hurts me greatly; I excuse all sins, try to make amends for them . . . How could one not be hurt on seeing the children who forget their Father, who do not love him . . . who do not know him?

This suffering on behalf of those who forget God, and on behalf of the God whom they have forsaken, impels Rafael—such is his fellowship—to offer his life in reparation:

If we truly love God, we must be hurt on seeing so many who do not even know him . . . If someone tells you that religious are selfish and that they think only of their own salvation . . . you tell that person that you know a Trappist who asks nothing for himself and who has dedicated his life to God in order to make reparation for the many offenses of people against him . . . Could I but make reparation to some extent for the great misdeeds of people against you . . . I would be content.

And if Rafael seems to express a rather negative judgement about all of humanity, about civilization and progress, about all human activity, whose "noise" rises to heaven but does not reach God because he rejects it, it is necessary to read the paragraph in which he mentions it all in the context of this booklet, *The Trappist's Apologia*. At this particular point he wants to emphasize the value of prayer, which ought to influence people's activity at all times. Rafael considers "that poor little, uncultured, mere Lay Brother, who quietly prayed and repeated the 'Hail Mary' there in his fraternity, to have contributed more for world peace than all the addresses made at the League of Nations since it began."

In addition to God, Rafael sees also the remedy for the social injustice and evils of his time, over which state of things every Christian ought to grieve. Here is a long passage that can be regarded as important with regard to the "pacifism" that was characteristic of Rafael, who moreover belonged to a rather high social class:

> If those at the top forget God, is it any wonder that those at the bottom are rebelling? . . . What is needed is not to go to the poor to preach patience and submission to them, but to go to the rich to tell them that if they are not just and do not give what they should, God's wrath will come down on them . . . The more God is banished from society, the greater the misery, and if among a people that calls itself Christian, people hate each other because of caste and self-interest, and if they separate themselves into rich and poor districts, what will happen on the day God's name is cursed by one class and the other? . . . Once the remembrance of God is stolen from the poor, they have nothing; their despair is justified, their hatred for the rich is inevitable, their longing for revolution and anarchy is logical; and if the rich find the thought of God a nuisance, and pay no heed to the precepts of the Gospel and the teachings of Jesus . . . then, they should not complain, and if their selfishness prevents their having anything to do with the poor, they should not be surprised if the latter endeavor to take their property by force. When I reflect that all social strife, all disputes would be done away with if only we looked to God a little . . . When I reflect, on seeing the show that people make of themselves, that the hatred and the envy, the selfishness and the lies would disappear if only we looked to God.[1]

---

1. Rafael seems here to be glimpsing the revolution, which was not long in breaking out in Oviedo, in early October.

Homesickness for La Trappe and helping his own family

Obviously Rafael's view of the outside world differs from the usual one. It has been remarked already that he views everything taking God into account, which could not fail to make him realize what a contrast there is between the reality that surrounds him and the life he had led in the monastery:

> How difficult it is, now that after being a Trappist I am in the outside world, to express the impression I get! . . . It is so difficult and diverse, so many things provide me with motives for meditation . . . Often without wanting to I compare my life as a novice in Citeaux with the life that surrounds me . . . It differs completely: in the way of doing, thinking, regarding! Priorities are not the same, God seems to be far away . . . at least, so it seems to me, even if such is not the case.

One thing that makes for severe homesickness for La Trappe, when contrasted with the life that is now his lot, is silence. It is in these circumstances that Rafael gives expression to his famous remark about silence: "Brother, do not make noise, I am speaking with God." When in the *Apologia* Rafael describes Trappist silence, he does so in particular by placing it over against the noise he has to put up with in the world outside:

> Since I left my La Trappe all I have to listen to is noise . . . The only music that does not disturb me is the sound of prayer . . . But one hears only a little of it in the outside world . . . All the rest is noise. Many ask me about the silence of La Trappe, and I do not know what to answer, for the silence of La Trappe is not silence . . . it is a sublime concert that the world outside does not understand . . . It is the silence of the body that allows the soul to enjoy the contemplation of God. It is not the silence of one who has nothing to say, but the silence of one who, having many and very beautiful things within, keeps quiet in order that mere words, which are always soiled, may not adulterate one's dialogue with God . . . In a word: silence is all in the contemplative life. On that account, now that I am in the outside world, all that is not silence seems but noise to me, and at times an intrusion.

Once clearly aware of Rafael's opinion, it is easy to understand what he says to two monks of his monastery:

It is as if you and I were not living on the same planet . . .
Seeing myself separated from you all makes my stay in the
world outside seem as if I were on loan and out of place . . .
I believe that I would never be able to cope were it not for the
absolute confidence I have that God will bring me once again
to the monastery . . . and because I know that I am doing his
will; otherwise my life would prove impossible.

He was to experience a still greater contrast during the tragic
days of October 1934 in the city of Oviedo, when revolutionary
forces terrorized the city with bombings, arson, general strike,
religious persecution, etc. Having left the monastery because of
God's design of purifying and putting his soul's stamina to the
test, he proved himself a comfort to his family in all the troubles
it went through at this time. As early as August of that year Rafael
was able to render great service and patient encouragement to his
very elderly grandaunt, who lived with his parents, by helping
her to make a good death. Now, in this tragic situation, his serene
and great Christian courage enabled Rafael to bring peace and
protection to all his family. Here are a few paragraphs from a long
letter, written by Rafael's mother on October 22, to members of
her family, describing the tragic days just experienced, which she
recalls as a frightful nightmare, during which Rafael's personal
and moral support was outstanding:

On Friday, October 5 . . . at half-past nine, the riot squad set
up their first machine-gun in front of our house on the principal side of the square, a strategic point from which to shoot
and at which to get supplies of ammunition . . . all day people who passed were stopped and searched . . . At six in the
evening my son Rafael, not wishing to omit his daily visit to
the friary of Saint Dominic, went out, leaving us worried at
the bad way things were looking. Then at seven, the shooting began, and all the people in the street fled . . . At last, at
seven-thirty he [Rafael] knocked at the front door, which had
been locked, and had to press the door-bell without lifting his
arms, for the police were shooting in all directions . . . The following night they burned down the friary, and killed five Do-
minicans . . . Bullets have pierced walls, leaving huge holes,
and have destroyed window-panes and doors; but we have
been spared . . . Yes . . . our house has been spared, although

so many have been destroyed, and we ourselves have been spared, although so many innocent people have been killed and tortured . . . How did we not die of dread and distress, and how did we manage to escape the fire that so surrounded us on all sides that almost the whole block was ablaze . . . enveloping us in all the smoke and suffocating us in the horrendous heat of flames that seemed to reach to the heavens amid explosions of oil and petrol tanks in garages and warehouses? . . . I know well who has freed us from the death that threatened us on all sides . . . My Trappist angel, whom God allowed leave his La Trappe in order to become our safeguard . . . ! He, who needed so much care and nourishment, spent those days without either food or sleep, giving us encouragement and assuring us that no harm would befall us, and that God was with him . . . How wise God's plans are . . . ![2]

Mentioning the excesses committed during those nine days of revolution, what with machine guns, dynamite, fires and the ceaseless threat offered by pistols and rifles, Rafael on October 25 would sorrowfully say, "For a few days I have witnessed the unbridled hatred of people. . . My mind has been horrified during these days; I never thought it possible that people could kill and destroy with so much fury."

After those days of so much tension, full of nervous strain and lacking the care that his illness required, Rafael was sent by his parents to Burgos, to rest and recuperate at the home of his uncle Alvaro and aunt Pepita for a month. His illness, from which before he had recovered so amazingly, now at times showed signs of a relapse, which called for further doses of insulin. On November 21, while passing through Venta de Baños on his way to rejoin his parents, Rafael paid a visit to the monastery. Father Marcelo, the Novice Master, had written to him, inquiring as to what had happened to him and his family during the days of revolution at Oviedo. Rafael wished to greet him and to explain

2. Later on Rafael himself would seem to accept the interpretation his mother gives of these events when, because of his second departure from the monastery owing to the Civil War, he tells her, "Who knows? . . . , God's bringing me out of La Trappe has a purpose, and it is evident that I have to be in the outside world at times when it is less fun . . . Do you remember October?" Rafael certainly refers here to the revolution in Oviedo just described by his mother.

in person how things were going with his illness, and that there had been a relapse.

Both the Abbot and the Father Master, when replying to Rafael's honest account of his condition, told him that the wisest thing to do was to wait for some time longer in order to verify whether his health would improve. This meant a wait without a date, for an indefinite time, which would lessen whatever hope there was of his returning to the novitiate. For Rafael was not yet fit to return to the monastery. His being with his family would continue the beneficial and decisive influence he had on them, of which he perhaps was not aware; it would at the same time prove both a help and an encouragement during a further trial for his family.

His sister, Mercedes, became seriously ill, and her parents brought her to Madrid for a course of radiotherapy. Rafael, his mother and his sister settled in Torrelodones near the capital, where he proved himself helpful to both of them during that long and terrible illness. Completely devoted to his sister, Rafael would humor her even to excess, amusing her during her long hours of suffering with his jokes and yarns, choosing and reading for her the books that would most cheer her, drawing funny figures and caricatures to make her laugh. It did not bother him in the least to go to Madrid at any hour of the day in order to satisfy some whim or other of hers, having ever a ready smile and loving words to lessen so much suffering. "I would like to suffer in her place," he would say as he tenderly looked at her, praying meanwhile to the Lord that such might be the case:

> I would ask the Lord to send me all those pains, send me suffering, and give rest to my sister either in this life or the next . . . To see someone suffering is awful. I grieve more over seeing someone suffer than over suffering myself . . . The Lord knows well what he is doing.

One day the sick girl became so ill that their mother asked Rafael to go quickly to Madrid and fetch the specialist that was attending his sister. The doctor refused to visit her; he thought there was nothing he could do, that she would inevitably die soon. Some days later, as night was falling, the sick girl's pains increased, and she asked Rafael to implore God to take her as soon as possible. He replied, "Take it easy, child; this very minute I am going to church, and will tell the Virgin to rid mother and you of all this suffering; you will have a good night; you will see."

He took the car in order to return sooner. After a quarter of an hour he came into the room happy and smiling, and quite simply told his sister, "That's that. I have just said to the Virgin, 'Mother dear, do see what you can do for my mother; make my sister well.' Now you will see how the Virgin will make you well." At eleven that night the last injection of morphine was given, and, what was unusual, she needed no further one, but slept the whole night through, unlike so many sleepless nights before that. Her pains disappeared completely, and a month and a half later Rafael's sister had regained the fifty-five pounds' weight she had lost. The holy Virgin had indeed listened to Rafael's prayer, which seemed so normal to him that he made little of it. He had good reason to remark not long after, "[the Virgin] loves me very much and never refuses me anything." After the sudden cure of his sister, Rafael stayed with her and their mother for the three months they were at Torrelodones, with a view to his own recovery. Early in October he came to Avila, where he stayed for the rest of that month.

The request for entrance as an oblate

It was from Avila that Rafael, after being away from his La Trappe for a year and a half, wrote to the Abbot requesting readmission. It was also from Avila that he had written for admission the first time. In his letter, the result of long prayer and reflection before the tabernacle, Rafael opened his heart to his superiors[3] to let them know not only his decision but also what had been happening in his soul. During the preceding year he had written little, and this letter, full of information, clearly shows his spiritual state.

During his first few months outside the monastery Rafael wrote copiously about his life in La Trappe and his leaving it, and crowned it all with his booklet *The Trappist's Apologia*, completed

---

3. He thought that Father Marcelo, his Father Master, was sick, but in fact he had died a few days earlier on October 1.

in October 1934. But after that the writings during all this next year of his life are actually few,[4] which is rather surprising given his tendency to write and the good it did him. Why, he did not even keep up his frequent correspondence with his monastery after his latest, brief visit on November 21, 1934, during which he was advised to postpone his return. On February 21, 1935, he wrote only a single letter, one to his Father Master, after being visited at his home in January of that year by the Abbot, and receiving a letter from the novices. What is the meaning of this silence on Rafael's part? Had he already forgotten his monastery? As Rafael's letter just mentioned makes clear, this was not the reason, although the monks could have thought so.

An examination of all that he wrote at this time indicates a Rafael who is suffering. This was nothing new in his life, but this time his suffering has been something special in its being much marked by doubt, uncertainty and darkness. In his letter to the Father Master, Rafael tells him:

> I have to tell you that I have had a great deal of trouble with nerves . . . Because of what? Father, I do not know; be it due to everything or to nothing . . . My morale and state of mind have been such that, as I say, I have not been able to write, and have preferred to weep a little without letting it be known . . . To say that I have not suffered would be telling a lie. Possibly you can understand why I have not written; knowing that I am loved by all of you, why should I disturb your peace with my griefs and groans?[5]

Although Rafael still regards Trappist life as the life for him, during this time he shows himself hesitating about returning to the monastery, as if the Lord wanted to detach him even from the certainty he at one time so often felt. No doubt the fact that his illness had not disappeared despite the time allowed posed a serious question for Rafael about his monastic vocation:

4. From October 1934 to October 1935.

5. Later on Rafael would explain this difficult period in his life, a time when he wrote so little, by the following principle: "Silence is where a monk finds the balm for his suffering and for his infrequent sense of desolation."

Lord, what do you want from me? . . . Here I am far from my
monastery, while every day that passes makes me ever more
lovingly homesick for it; as far as I am concerned, life for me
is there, and, while well aware of time passing, I do not know
what God wants from me . . . At times I am inclined to think
that really I do not deserve to be a child of Citeaux, and that
my dream has been too exalted for my poor self, that God has
humbled and punished me . . . Maybe I committed the sin of
pride, and I assure you, Father, that I am indeed expiating it.

Rafael interprets his present darkness and desolation in the
light of his personal experience of sensing himself to be a sinner, a notion that often appears in his writings at this time. He
regards the darkness and uncertainty that he is going through
as a result of his sin:

[He] was hiding himself from me . . . as I well deserved, since
my sins have not been few . . . Now I can see that I am a
miserable wretch, miserly with his love . . . and only slightly
in accord with his will . . . I am weak . . . I am sin . . . I am
nothing. Lord, I am a poor sinner who neither praises nor glo-
rifies you . . . I would give you all that I had, but all that I had
were sins, wretchedness and imperfections.[6]

Nonetheless, despite this unpleasant experience of coming
to regard himself as sin, he is internally moved to hope in God,
and to such an extent as to entrust his very sins to him in an act
of total confidence:

6. Possibly his long-drawn out illness is affecting Rafael's psychological
state, with the further effect of inducing the uncertainty that now afflicts him,
and which he puts down to his sins. Those who knew him intimately were quite
sure that he never lost his baptismal innocence. No doubt his feeling himself
a sinner is the result of his growing awareness of the greatness of God. Rafael
himself, going on his own experience, would say as much when he later wrote
that "in the spiritual life, in the interior life . . . there is nothing except God, and
however one may regard oneself, one is forever, on reflection, seeing oneself as
so tiny, so minute and insignificant . . . so much nothing in his presence that all
that remains in one's soul is a sense of the immensity and greatness of God . . .
a feeling in the presence of which the soul would like not to see itself, to disappear, to neither be nor exist . . . How great God is and how small and wretched
we are!"

Lord, do not look away from your servant, who, although a
sinner, hopes to be able, thanks to your mercy, to gaze on you
for all eternity. I entrust myself completely to you . . . I want
to be all yours; I give you even my sins, the very last thing I
own as exclusively mine.

This great act of confidence is undoubtedly the fruit of love.
For the fact of the matter is that Rafael, at the very time he has
the forceful and ruthless experience of feeling himself a sinner,
experiences also that his heart is on fire with love for God, who
continues to be his all. Such is the interior interaction between
the love God has placed in his heart and the personal limitation
of his own poverty and sin, seen of course in the light of God's
closeness and absolute holiness:

Listen, [Lord] to my heart . . . Without sounds or words it
knows how to tell you all my love for you and all that you
mean to me . . . My light, my guide, my only love, my dream,
my only reason for living . . . for were I to lose you, Lord, my
life would be extinguished like a flame without oxygen, for
you are my breath, the air that I breathe and the bread that I
eat . . . Do you want me to love you more, although my heart
is so tiny? . . . Do me the favor of making it big and generous,
that I may be all heart in order to be all yours and love you
much . . . You can do it if you want to . . . Tone down the
longing that I have, otherwise I cannot live. My soul is full to
overflowing. You have put so much love in my soul, that soul,
Lord, which is so tiny and wretched. If it is you, Lord, who
inflict the wound, do in all kindness stop the bleeding as well;
but do not leave me in this state, for I cannot endure it.

And this state of desolation, which was certainly painful,
Rafael has had to live through all on his own. No one was at hand
to help him discern the real state of his soul, in which the Lord
was at work even then. Rafael says so himself, although with a
certain longing for the confessor that he had in the monastery:

Most of the time that I have spent outside La Trappe I have
been able to discuss intimate matters only with God . . . At
times I feel that I am all alone and that all have forsaken me
. . . I often think (of my confessor). I have so very frequently

found myself all alone in my doubts that I have had plenty to
offer to God—even if, in reality, it is all so little.

The sense of being a sinner that he has experienced so intensely could only fill Rafael with a vivid sense of humility, even
if he would say that he was not very humble. Humility, in fact,
has been gaining ground in his heart because of the humiliation
involved in the acceptance of his actual condition, both physical
and spiritual, as Rafael himself realizes:

> God has sent me an illness . . . in order to humble me . . .
> Well, then, humble yourself . . . I used to think that I had be-
> gun to be good, and it was no such thing; I am where I used
> to be, and maybe lower still. I do not deserve the affection you
> all have for me, nor that you should remember me.

And it would seem that it was precisely humility that helped
Rafael to write to the Abbot requesting readmission. There can
be no doubt that it was through humility that he overcame the
conflict he went through at this time, a conflict that it seemed the
passage of time would not overcome and that made him unsure
about his vocation. On the one hand lay the great attraction he
felt for the monastic life to which he believed himself called;
and on the other hand, the continuance of his illness, which,
despite temporary improvement and assurances about a cure,
still demanded, at the very time he was writing to the Abbot, a
special diet and medicine and a lifestyle more or less at variance
with regular monastic observance—yes, quite incompatible. So
Rafael bethought himself of a middle course: he would offer to
enter as an "oblate." Given the exceptions to the regular routine
of the monastery that his way of life would entail, exceptions all
the more humbling for an exquisitely sensitive young man like
Rafael, it was only humility that enabled him to consider, above
all to accept, and ultimately to maintain this lifestyle.

Nonetheless, prepared by his recent experience of personal
poverty, he feels that he has, thanks to humility, the strength to
live in the lowly condition of an oblate, as he expressly says in
his letter to the Abbot:

> Reverend Father, you may tell me of the humiliation that being
> a nobody and nothing means; but am I of some account? As

for humiliation itself, I think I will not feel it, since to humble someone it is necessary to make one descend from above, and I consider that I do not need to descend at all; real humiliation, on the contrary, is to make a creature ascend in the sight of others, since when one sees oneself as one is before God, such an utter wretch in God's sight and made so much of in front of others . . . then indeed does one experience humiliation.

Rafael is ready to accept, with pleasure and gladness, being a nobody in the monastery. He must accept even not giving the good example of observing the rule. Not only that, he will accept the unusual and humiliating fact, following a suggestion of his own, that his father offer a sum of money to the monastery to prevent his being a burden to the community.[7]

Because he feels that God wants him for himself alone, he is willing to renounce the dreams and desires he had when he entered the monastery for the first time. This he makes plain in the letter where he asks for readmission, as follows:

I do not deserve to be a monk . . . To chant Holy Mass? . . . Lord, what does it matter if I am going to see you very soon? As for vows, do I not love God with all my strength? So, why add vows? Lack of all that will not prevent my being close to him, devoting my silence with others to him, and loving him quietly, humbly, as a mere oblate . . . You, Reverend Father, can count on having an oblate whose only longing is to give God glory, to love him, to serve him with a heart that wants nothing, and even makes a present to him of the desire to be professed, for God demands this of him, and, believe me, I do so without forcing myself, with pleasure and gladness.

And he accepts it all with love, because of the love that, as we have seen, flames in his heart, a love that has been purified in the course of time, or rather, by the action of God, which explains his telling the Abbot:

---

7. Although Rafael's father agreed to contribute a monthly sum to defray the expenses that Rafael's illness imposed on the monastery, Father Fernando, Rafael's brother, mentioned in 1980 that such a contribution was never in fact made. But that does not lessen in any way the humiliating condition that Rafael suggested and accepted in order to enter the monastery for the second time.

Reverend Father, I remember your telling me, when I entered the monastery, that God would reward me even in this life for the sacrifice I was making . . . Well, by now God knows well that I do not follow God for anything like that . . . I love God because I do, full stop. True, my love for God is nothing much, but my love is not self-centered; I know that he loves me and that is enough for me.

No doubt the Abbot understood the dispositions and desires that Rafael made clear in his letter, the great work that the Lord was bringing about in him. For before he left Avila, Rafael received the letter that readmitted him to the community of San Isidoro. A new stage in his life had begun.

V

WAITING TO REENTER

Waiting and writing

On November 4, 1935, Rafael reached Oviedo, where he would remain until he entered the monastery for the second time, on January 11, 1936. During all this time his copious correspondence, particularly with his aunt, the Duchess of Maqueda, is quite surprising, not least when compared with the time previous to his request for readmission to the monastery, days remarkable for how silent he was, as has been described. Now, how to account for this intense correspondence?

While he and his mother and sister had stayed at Avila, Rafael had talked a great deal with his aunt. In one of his letters he reminds her how, when they were together in the car, she would ask him to speak to her about God. Spiritual friendship had so developed between them that, in addition to family ties, they had come to regard themselves as sister and brother. Well aware that Rafael had been very helpful to her, so much so that she had wept when he left Avila, she begs him now to help her from Oviedo to become holy. Although unable to understand how the Lord could have chosen him to help his aunt, he agrees quite simply to her request, telling her, "You already have all that I am and am able to do," which will enable him to repay his aunt for the help she had given him before he entered the monastery the first time. This Rafael acknowledges with great candor:

> The Lord has arranged for me to come your way; it must be for some purpose. Am I able to help you? Well, I do help you . . . I am nobody and nothing; possibly I am only a step in the staircase that God has given you to enable you to go higher . . .

> God used both of you [aunt and uncle] to plant a seed in me
> that gradually germinated. If only I could repay something of
> what I owe you. I shall always remember our chats at Pedrosil-
> lo, during which I too kept telling you trifles, and you with
> such great kindness enabled me to see the Lord, and I learned
> so much. It is not the other way round now . . . but I never
> even dreamed that I could pay you back in the same coin.

The correspondence between them at this period was so intense and frequent that Rafael would tell his aunt, "Your letters
are my only occupation these days." And to such an extent that
his own family could not help noticing it:

> Here at home they are not surprised that you write to me and
> I answer . . . Often my mother has asked me what you are
> telling me . . . and I have told her the truth . . . that you had
> great trust in me; kept telling me of your *spiritual difficulties*,
> and I, responding to such trust and *doing whatever I could*,
> would reply in order to help you to love God . . . Which
> seems to those here quite normal. One day Leopoldo asked
> me if I was translating *Don Quixote* into Greek . . . They have
> never seen me write so much.

Rafael has accepted his aunt's request that he speak to her
about God since he is aware that his God-given mission, while
living in the outside world, is to help others love God. He has
good reason to tell his aunt, "Love moves my pen," and that he
puts into his letters much love for God, who, in addition, guides
his pen, and that were he able by means of his letters to bring light
and love for God to people, he would spend the rest of his life pen
in hand. However, any help that he may be able to offer her will
come from his own experience, without any learned pretensions;
Rafael is well aware of the peripheral value of anything he might
be able to tell his aunt. He puts it this way when writing to her:

> I do not know whether I am good or bad when I try to share
> with you the lights that the Lord gives me . . . quite numer-
> ous though they be. My wish would be to put my whole soul
> before you on paper, and I am rather discouraged when I re-
> alize how poor my words are . . . My little contribution to
> something so great . . . I heartily send whatever you ask; do

not misuse it . . . Possibly you alone will understand this, and are the only person in the world whom I address this way; and I do so because I realize that, perhaps, it may do you some good, despite the fact that my love for God has always been hidden from the eyes of others.

Throughout this correspondence Rafael reveals his soul to his aunt as never before, which explains why these letters are of particular importance for knowing him at this time. He writes very trustingly, keeping no secrets, because from the first he tells his aunt to tear up his letters once she has read them, and later he repeatedly stresses the idea: "Tell me whatever you want to and as you want to; I understand you and, although I do not deserve your expectations, your letters will be read, answered and torn up. Do likewise with mine . . . With such trust as this, I write to you."

Such great trust and freedom enables Rafael to write without being fussy about his ideas; he writes whatever comes to mind, without any kind of revision, which explains what he means when he tells his aunt that he writes about what he has not given much thought to before, and that he finds it impossible to write about what he used to think, and that once he begins talking to her about God, he ends up talking to God, so that he uses his letters for meditation when talking about God and about the works of God in creatures and about his love. They are an opportunity to express the affections of his heart, encouraging his mind, leaving him in great peace, finding great consolation in it all.

Teaching the ways of the Spirit

Rafael, going on his own experience, proves himself in these letters an expert in the spiritual life. He understands that of his aunt, whose prayer and dispositions he is able to discuss, and he knows how to discern the importance of what she is going through in relation to its effect on her interior life. He is able to guide her and to inspire her; his skill extends even to pointing out to her, not without misgivings, where the greatest perfection lies, at times using for her guidance a discussion of what he has already experienced himself.

Knowing that "on the way up we tend to cut down on many things and take on others that are not necessary for ascending the mount of perfection," Rafael often invites his aunt to live a life of detachment; with it one flies better. She must also avoid looking at herself in order to go up to God, must be convinced that the less she looks at herself, the better she will see God. It is a case of the "not gathering flowers" mentioned by Saint John of the Cross, as they both agree, and it is the attitude that is "the summary of all this period" in Rafael's life, as he himself says. One must go "forward, without looking to either side, stripped of all else and without looking at ourselves . . . so ready that when the Bridegroom arrives we have our lamps well lit . . . Let us not bother about anything else." It is a matter of detachment which, welcomed with love, leads to God, even if we do not notice that it does so:

> Go forward; do not stop at your humility or you will stop at yourself . . . Do not stop at your littleness or you will stop at yourself . . . Go forward; go up to the Lord, for once you are with him, you will see how, as a result, you realize that you are nothing, and will love him without *being aware* of it yourself . . . Then indeed he will fill us completely. We will disappear and he will be all.

Rafael clearly states that the whole of the interior life is contained in and concentrated on love when he tells his aunt:

> All the interior life *boils down* to loving God more and more . . . Penitence, prayer, mortifying one's senses, etc . . . all of that is good, of course . . . but it seems to me that it is easier than all that *to confine yourself to obeying*, in a humble way, whatever the love for God that you have within you should indicate . . . *Everything comes* from love for God . . . You will see, once you make perfect the love that is your only interior life . . . how all the rest is of no importance. That same love will make you humble, mortified, charitable . . . will make you a saint . . . a saint because of love . . . A saint only and exclusively because of love.

Centered in love and "in waiting"

In actual fact, this stage in Rafael's life is characterized by love. An examination of all his writings at this period clearly proves the preponderant place Rafael gives to love. The proof is not just the number of times love is mentioned (even though Rafael at this time often brings the subject up); nor is it just that, together with references to the Virgin, love occupies (although very differently) a special place. Rather, it is an interior and intense disposition that makes him declare, "I want to occupy myself with only one thing: loving God; *with that alone . . .* If I only want to love . . . why do they not allow me to?"

The transformation wrought in Rafael is truly amazing. All of a sudden he is to be found in such a state of unitive love that he does not want to be engaged in other activities and exterior occupations that might hinder a single moment of being present to God through love. Owing to the silence that preceded this stage and the small number of writings available, it is difficult to follow his rapid spiritual development, the way by which he has reached this degree of unitive love; still, this is the way he is to be seen at this point. "Truly this soul is lost to everything and gained only for love, spiritually active in no other way," as Saint John of the Cross says in the *Spiritual Canticle.*[1]

In his desire to sustain himself only by love for God, Rafael, who certainly knows the Mystical Doctor, repeats his famous words, "To love is my only occupation."[2] He regards this interiorly experienced desire as an answer to his query about God's purpose for him. After all, God has given him a heart to love him, and his particular vocation, too, confirms his conviction about love, in the realization of which he finds both meaning and contentment in life. For this reason, Rafael believes that the ambition to love is not presumption. So he will later say:

> You must not think that it is pride or lack of humility to be ambitious for love . . . I clearly perceive that God has given me a heart for only two purposes: the first and most important being to love him and him alone . . . That is the only content-

1. Canticle B, stanza 28,1.
2. Ibid., stanza 28, 7-8.

ment in life . . . : to be on fire with love for God, knowing
that he is the God who is waiting for me . . . My life is my
vocation, and my vocation boils down to this: to love God. He
wants nothing more from me than that I love him, keep him
company . . . Not letting the flowers keep one back and going
forward is what the Lord wanted to show us.

It is a matter of going ahead without looking sideways, because love, being dynamic, will not allow one to delay; love itself
tends to grow: "How could we live at rest having what we have?
. . . No, it is not possible . . . We cannot love God more always
. . . We must not be satisfied with a little; and if some day we are
on fire with it . . . is not that what we are looking for?" This is a
love that tends toward encounter; and in his longing to discover
everywhere the presence of the Bridegroom who is slow to arrive, Rafael shows himself both impatient and contemplative at
one and the same time:

Everything tells me what you are, everything brings me to
you; but everything is but a faint reflection of your goodness,
of your love . . . and still, all of that is not you . . . When I go
for a walk, all I do is ask the valleys and the mountains and
all creatures . . . whether they have seen my Beloved . . . the
one I love most . . . How hidden is the Jesus I have! and with
what longing do I ask him to disclose his presence to me, even
if I cannot bear it and "his beauty kill" me!

Although Rafael knows that it is more perfect not to desire
anything, he cannot understand "how it is possible not to desire
to be already once and for all in body and soul with all that is . . .
in heaven," where we shall have sight of God. God is his life, and
he possesses him and experiences him so intimately within himself
that he is amazed and only knows how to love him greatly. God
draws him so strongly that he cannot stop still. Although feeling
impelled towards him, sometimes he senses God to be so far away
that he makes his own the words of Saint John of the Cross: "I know
not how I survive, without living there, where I am alive";[3] and the
Psalmist's, "How long will you hide your face?" (Ps 12:26):

3. Canticle B, stanza 8.

How long, O Lord . . . Living here is so awful . . . being so
far away, when the Lord could with a single glance snatch
us away once and for all, thus cutting short this life that is
one long longing for his love . . . in which thinking of him
does not bring rest . . . in which the heart is all agitation
and moves without hope of further rest. Would that the Lord
would either take it away once and for all, or so strengthen it
that we can bear up . . . Lord, living like this is not life; my
life is in you.

Possessing only the desire for God, even if he would like
to fly away, Rafael finds that everything still keeps him down,
yet he is willing to live "flattened . . . by the weight of a vast
love for God, one's heart rent by so much shouting in silence";
nevertheless, made strong by God to love him, he sustains his
waiting with the love and hope of one who knows himself sure
of a death which he welcomes with joy in order to have sight of
the Lord at last:

How drawn-out the waiting is . . . ! And yet how pleasant
waiting is for one who truly loves! When, for some reason or
another, I think of God, I am so overwhelmed that I regard
death as a trifle. For a Trappist, the contentment of living consists in the sure hope of dying . . . The thought that one will
die very soon in order to have sight of God . . . is really glad
excitement in the heart of a monk . . . All our wisdom consists in knowing how to wait.

Talking about Mary

It is at this time that Rafael tells us that "when all is said and
done, the life of a monk of Citeaux is nothing else than God and
the Virgin. He is busy about that, on that he lives . . . What else,
then, is there to talk about?" Because of that it is not surprising
that, continuing to regard himself as a Trappist, he devotes a great
part of his writings to the Virgin, who, together with mention of
God, is to be found all over them from start to finish.

In his letters at this time there are at least 340 references to Mary.[4] His devotion to the Virgin at the time of his spiritual transformation is very noticeable, even if it is not new. He had learned it in the monastery: "Before this I too did not know what devotion to Mary meant . . . but in La Trappe they taught me to love her greatly, and since then I want the whole world to know and reverence her . . ."[5]

And from the time he really began to love Mary, Rafael resolved "not to write anything to anyone without mentioning the Virgin at least once." In his letters at this time, he often shows his desire to make her known, saying this explicitly to his aunt when intending to help her spiritually, sure that she would soon experience the effects of her devotion:

> I have decided that you are to love the Lady, because I can see that that is the first thing that you must do to become a saint . . . and since you have such a long way to go, the speediest way to *begin* to love God is to love his Mother . . . After a very short time you will notice that you love her wholeheartedly; nothing less would do. You will begin to notice its effects . . . You will see how well, with the help of the most holy Virgin, we will get to wherever we should; do not forget this.

Here, too, Rafael is writing about his own experience: he has had much experience of the Virgin's help; she "never lets one down." So he expects everything from her, feels somewhat crazy about Mary and is inclined to write a lot about her, ever repeating the same message about the Lady, as he sometimes calls her. Mary had, in fact, influenced Rafael's spiritual life in a special way, which enables him to discuss her role in the Christian life. As Mediatrix, she purifies and presents our prayer to God, together with our love and the offering of our life. Sometimes she is the direct object of Rafael's prayer: she is able to help us in our

4. In at least 44 of these allusions the Virgin is closely linked to God or Jesus. Examples of these are: "I have asked the Lord and Mary": "The Virgin looks at you and God helps you"; "I find rest in Him and in Mary": "in Jesus and Mary": "May Mary enlighten us and Jesus give us his grace," etc.

5. Later on, remembering his years as a sodalist at his Jesuit college, he would say, "I too am very grateful to the Jesuit Fathers for introducing us in our early years to devotion to Mary."

efforts at reforming our own character, in the temptations that come from our rebellious nature and in all the struggles that are part of our present life; she drives away the spirit of evil, freeing us from all fright and filling our lives with joy. She gives us the confidence that prevents our floundering amid the squalls and storms, enabling us to know what we ought to do, for, as Rafael says expressly to his aunt, "even in the darkest squalls of this world, if you raise your eyes to the Virgin . . . you will be able to see to some extent." The fact is that the Virgin has been his only comfort during the almost two years he has spent outside the monastery, above all during particularly difficult moments when leaving his La Trappe and later on.

He had every reason to write:

> Mary is so kind! . . . the Virgin is so good! There is no pain that she does not assuage, no contentment that she does not sanctify . . . Nothing is difficult when she is present . . . Everything comes out well; everything is easy, even being a saint . . . I assure you that if we always had recourse to Mary, we ourselves would be very different . . . I have always found it very helpful . . . If only you could see it, I owe her everything . . . My vocation, my health, little or great, I take care of for God and for Mary . . .[6]

This explains why Rafael, who holds that if he were not grateful to the Virgin, "he would not even deserve to breathe," would go so far as to say that doing "all for her and through her is little enough."

Meanwhile he is so convinced of the importance of the Virgin's function and love that in a letter at this time he does not hesitate to state that he is going to La Trappe in order to love Mary on behalf of those who do not know her.

---

6. Rafael's aunt, who had grasped the richness of his message about the Virgin, asked him to write something about the Virgin and publish it. Rafael, replying to her request in his letter of December 4, 1935, put off doing it until he was once more in La Trappe, provided the Abbot gave him permission. Once back in the monastery, however, he never published anything, which was only to be expected in the monastic climate of those days when publishing was a rare event, not least for a mere oblate.

Reasons for reentering

Nonetheless, his love for Mary is not the only reason given by Rafael for returning soon to the monastery. During the last few years he has noticed that the Lord has made his vocation more and more definite, even when he did not advert to the fact, and he has to admit that his leaving the monastery was a great good fortune. So now he sees his way quite simply: "Fullest love for God and silence with people." He offers himself to God, offers his very blood "in order to help people *in whatever way possible*, the people of the whole world, that they may love God, without being aware of him." Yes, he does want "to be forgotten by the world and by people . . . , so that he may silently offer himself to God in the lowliness of an oblate's habit," an offering on behalf of all:

> "Oblate" means . . . an offering . . . I offer Him what I am and as I am, good or bad, with or without my health; my life, my body, my soul, my heart, all . . . absolutely all. I have offered myself for all: for my parents, my brothers and sister; for missionaries, priests . . . for those who are suffering, and for those who offend Him.

Here then, the apostolic motivation of Rafael's second entering at La Trappe is made clear. His reentering, like his first entering, is in response to the Lord who calls him, and he surrenders his whole being in the search for God; but this is complemented by an apostolic dimension for the benefit of others. Rafael's spiritual maturity includes an apostolate, although it is carried out in the solitude and silence of the monastery. He who had exercised a discreet apostolate among his family during his time outside the monastery, and who was by now better acquainted with human reality, thanks to his new vision through "God's prism," could not forget the help due from him to all, least of all when leaving once again for the monastery, from where he could exercise the influence of his faith and love.[7] The note of universality in his

---

7. This apostolic bent is displayed when Rafael writes to his father from the monastery, with regard to the difficult times Spain was living through, "Now Spain asks our prayers, sacrifices and penances; with ardor we give them to her." And again, "Do not think I have forgotten you; you are very present to me

silent apostolate is a fresh aspect of his spiritual life, the result of the development he has experienced in it.

In his new attempt to live at La Trappe, which "is nothing other than this: love for God," Rafael again hopes—as he did the first time—to reach sanctity. He says so expressly: "I am going to La Trappe to become a saint." Despite sensing so much going on in his soul, and not knowing what exactly is happening to him, he does nonetheless clearly perceive a strong desire for holiness, a desire that he wants to realize with haste: "I have . . . some crazy desires to become a saint. Nor can I be satisfied with a little . . . [nothing will do but] a high peak . . . One has to become a saint." This ambitious desire, which he accepts as a gift to him from God, a gift from the Lord who so greatly enlightened him, makes him feel as if afraid, but only because he is not going along with what the Lord is giving him. He puts it like this: "I know that if I went along with the graces and suggestions of God, I would already be a saint . . . I see that the way ahead is very long . . . while I am only at the beginning and make no contribution of my own."

The struggle during the last few moments

Rafael experiences his frailty, his personal poverty during the few days that precede his reentering the monastery, in the "*tedious taking leave* of everything" that he has to go through. Only a few of his days in the outside world remain, but they "are the most difficult of all," and although the Virgin supports him, he asks for the prayerful help of his aunt and of the monks at this point when "he is battling against many things."

Although convinced that he has to go to La Trappe, he finds it hard to leave home, even if, in another way, it is just what he desires. "This conflict," he says, "presses on me from all sides." He reveals with great honesty the feelings of his heart, the great struggle that is going on within him:

---

at many moments. I intend to help parents, brothers and sister . . . as you may suppose . . . I ask Her [Mary] to enlighten you, to give you faith, to make you holy in the midst of the world . . . " convinced that by prayer "we can accomplish more than by all the din of words that we could imagine."

What I am about to do is such a pretty gesture for the world outside . . . ! The heroic looks so good when done with a smile . . . ! But, look . . . underneath all that *show* there are, at times, very bitter tears; crosses that the world is unaware of, which I carry badly, dragging them along. Underneath all that there is nothing but wretchedness . . . underneath this going-to-La Trappe gesture of mine, which the world thinks I perform with extraordinary pleasure and only for love for God, I carry the human being that *I am*, with loathing for the haircloth and the most awful repugnance for the discipline . . . I carry with me stuff that is in revolt . . . , a heart that suffers greatly on seeing the suffering about me and that has much love for my parents and the brothers and sister whom I must leave . . . "

Rafael has always believed that to grow in love for God one must not refuse to struggle, cost what it may, in order to go forward "struggling with ourselves to banish the *I* that does us so much harm." Now, in the face of his interior struggle before re-entering La Trappe, he tells us:

I must walk over my own self in order to go to God; I make an act of love for Him, and all is over . . . It is necessary [to do so] . . . I only want to love God; I only want to so surrender myself to Him that even my breathing itself be for Him.

Overcoming his interior struggle by love, two days before leaving for the monastery, he can joyfully tell his mother, "I am going to La Trappe . . . but very pleased to do so, since I am 'seeking my Love,' as the poem of Saint John of the Cross says."[8] And since Rafael does not regret giving himself entirely to God— his decision to go to La Trappe—he tells us that "I would do it a thousand times over if I had a thousand lives."

8. Canticle B, stanza 3.

VI

FROM HERE TO THERE

In the monastery once again

After spending a day at Avila to take leave of his uncle and aunt, Rafael, accompanied by his father and his brother Leopoldo, arrives at the monastery on January 11, 1936, to live there as an oblate.

Once again he has to say good-bye to those he loves so much. Once again he has to leave his usual comforts and cigarettes at the door of the monastery. In addition, this time he has to forego the pleasure he had of success in his discreet apostolate among his relatives.[1] He must also, on a day to day basis, do without the warm welcome that the late Father Marcelo would always give him, and must accept the new Father Master, who has not shown himself exactly enthusiastic and prompt when corresponding with Rafael in connection with the latter's re-entry.[2]

Still, he is ready for everything, unwilling to yield at any point of his upward journey to the God who calls him so persistently. Whatever needs to be curbed, he cuts out; he steadily transforms whatever needs to be corrected; whatever has to be added, he includes little by little with strong constancy, convinced that God's ways are easy and straightforward to negotiate "once one walks

---

1. Above all, Rafael had to renounce the apostolate by correspondence that he had been exercising, in particular with his aunt, to whom he would scarcely write at all from the monastery.

2. In fact, Rafael had to write with some urgency to Father José Olmedo, the new Novice Master, a second time on January 7, when he did not get a reply to his letter of January 3, requesting some definite information about his reentry. Even if Rafael shows himself somewhat impatient for a reply, it seems certain, as some witnesses noted, that Father José did not like Rafael very much.

them with steady purpose and a heart that is free and fixed on Him." To this he applies his will wholly and perseveringly in order to respond to the Lord. Rafael has renounced everything, leaving "what is nothing in order to have what is everything." He has given everything back to God and as a reward for his total empti-ness, he will come to possess the fullness mentioned by mystical writers, a process of which he himself was aware: "Believe me, brother, everything created brings us to God, but it is not God. People at times bring us to Him . . . Possibly our desires, when they are holy, do so as well; but as long as one's heart is not empty and solitary, the immensity of God cannot enter it."

This time Rafael is not entering, as he did the first time, full of life, health and dreams, glad to be just another of the monks who work and fast, rise early and keep strictly to the Rule of Saint Benedict. Now he is a sick person who needs special medicine and care. But this is of no importance to him. Unable to follow the Rule strictly, he has renounced his own most legitimate aspi-rations, including giving the good example of exact observance, as already mentioned.

Of the Brother Rafael, jealous lover of the monastery and of its usages, thrilled with all that constituted life in the novitiate when he entered it in 1934, nothing remains. He can write, "In La Trappe, La Trappe and Trappists count least," and, when speaking explicitly and in all candor of the change that has been wrought in him, "as for the picture that I admired years ago . . . things are different today . . . Now, with Mary's help, I can see that what is of chief importance in a Trappist monastery is God . . . All my impressions . . . have by now given place to one sole essential, the essential that was lacking before: God."[3]

His desires, his God-given impatience, his disquiet, have been wiped out or, better, have been transformed by the process of purification which the Lord put him through when he left the monastery, a process he regards as a great mercy from God to him, since it opened the eyes of his soul and enabled him to know himself, "to get rid of much self-love and to bless God."

---

3. This is why Rafael would tell his uncle, "Do not come looking for La Trappe, but for the God of La Trappe, for . . . although a creature is good when it is from God, God is better."

Referring to himself in the third person, Rafael would later say, "Everything was transformed; and in order that nothing of *what was before* should remain, his way of judging changed as well."

His soul had needed to be purified from the imperfections that hindered his ascending the high and mysterious peaks of his union with God or, as he would say, "it is necessary and has been necessary to put everything aside in order to breathe a little," which made it possible for him, going on the experience of his own detachment, to tell his uncle later, "I have asked for many things for you; but above all for one . . . : detachment from everything and from everyone, that the Lord may fill you fully; that in forgetting the created, you may think only of the Creator."[4]

Thanks to the purification process and to the detachment he has attained, Rafael is happy amid whatever humiliation and cross his present sick condition may suppose. And he is happy because he has God, and having him, what more is there to desire? Health? That does not bother him now, since he has learned to enjoy his uselessness and regards his sickness as his treasure in this world, thanks to his spiritual unconcern.

This is the Rafael who has entered the monastery for the second time, who "hides himself from the outside world's eyes in order to meet his God." God is still the one sole reason not only for his monastic life but also for his very existence; because of God he does not want to waste a single minute of his life. He tries to see God in everything; in the presence of God's greatness, one loses oneself.

But not everything in his monastic life is a consolation. He resides and performs most of his duties in the monastery infirmary, and before long, the experience of belonging to a community and at the same time finding himself separated from his companions in the novitiate makes him feel interiorly troubled, and also to feel a heavy sadness. He says it this way to his aunt: "For the first few days, the infirmary refectory saddened me, as I am separated from my companions; but now I bless God from

4. Here Rafael alludes to the poem of Saint John of the Cross: "Forgetfulness of the created/ Remembrance of the Creator/ Attention to the interior/ And continual love for the Beloved."[Poem 14 in Spanish; Poem XXII in Allison Peers; last poem in Kavanagh-Rodriguez, but neither version has been used. —Trans.]

the depths of my heart: if he seems to treat us harshly . . . it only serves to show how wrong we are!"

Between consolation and desolation, Rafael finds that time flies continually, imperceptibly. Time enables him to adapt increasingly once again to ordinary community living, although he now has to exchange the hoe he would use in the fields in the afternoons with the novices, for the broom with which he sweeps in the infirmary; he now spends his mornings studying Latin, and later on philosophy. This particular time of the year also immerses him in Lent, his second in the monastery, with its greater restriction of correspondence and greater intensity of penitential practice. In addition, this time helps him to notice the gradual change that is coming over his life. He candidly tells his uncle and aunt about it: "If only you could see how I have changed during this month! . . . I am so grateful to the Lord for all that he does with me; I do not know where to hide . . . ! Believe me, brother, I have greatly changed in the way I think and judge."

Meditations of a Trappist and the Civil War

On July 12, 1936, Rafael began his *Meditations of a Trappist* copybook, a collection of "meditations, soliloquies, impressions" that he dedicated to the Virgin Mary. At the start of it, Rafael offers an apologia for this booklet, which is the result, above all, of his facility for writing, and writing about God:

> No matter when I take up the pen, something always turns up for me to say or tell . . . While it is certain that God asks me for silence with others, which I gladly offer to him . . . what he does allow me is to speak to him . . . he gives me a blank page and allows me to write.

On July 18, a few days after Rafael began to use his copybook, the Nationalist revolt broke out in Spain. On July 19, Rafael describes the reaction in the monastery to the news:

> I had just gone down to the church . . . when we were waiting in choir for Mass to begin, there was some commotion among the monks . . . Instead of three priests, only one came out [from the sacristy] . . . the bells were not rung and we merely

recited the Office . . . On leaving the church all we found out was that there is a revolution going on in Spain, that soldiers are to be seen on the roads and there is talk of an uprising.

Faced with such an emergency, the community of San Isidoro could not avoid feeling involved. Rafael clearly says so:

Now, in the situation prevailing in Spain, we Spanish monks cannot be unconcerned . . . and if, while the outside world is happy and amusing itself, we do not want to find out anything about it . . . now that it suffers and there is a war on, we want to know all about it and to help all concerned.

While the life of the monks in the monastery went on more or less as usual, as if there were no war, they were now well aware of many additional obligations, offering themselves to God for peace, praying particularly for it and "in order to ask for *something* that the world seems to lack." On a personal level, news of the tricky situation has helped Rafael to open himself still more to God and to grow in self-surrender to him. This self-surrender, already rather perceptible in some of his writings since reentering the monastery, he now makes evident by placing his life in God's care:

This is a difficult time; but why worry? Whoever has God lacks nothing, and no matter how great the harm people may do to us, the most they can do is take our lives . . . and a Trappist's life is of very little worth . . . Or, rather, of none at all. As far as I am concerned, of course, as long as I have life I shall use it in God's service, and when He, in whatever way, takes it from me, that will be fine, it is His, after all, and as His, He can do what He likes with it . . . I cannot understand a monk who fears death.[5]

Moreover, the urgency at this point in the history of his country gave Rafael a special reason for carrying out the hidden apostolate

5. Rafael here borrows from Saint Teresa's poem: "Let nothing bother you/ Nothing fluster you/ All is so passing/ God in unchanging/ Patience obtains everything/ Having God means lacking nothing/ Only God is fully satisfying" (Poem 6 in Spanish text).

that had moved him to reenter the monastery. Doing what was most accessible in his present circumstances, he prays for all and for Spain, well aware that he too can fight on from where he is, as with strong conviction he tells his uncle:

> It is enough for you to know that I too have my "battle-front," although it is without noise or flags or gunshot; and with the Virgin's help, I too fight for Spain . . . This poor Trappist oblate, in the silence of his seclusion, remembers those who struggle and fight, those who suffer and die, and since I cannot send you either soldiers or arms or money, which is what Spain is asking for . . . I send you my poor prayers; I send you the comfort of knowing that in the midst of the struggling people, there are those who raise their hearts to God.

Called up by his country, he leaves the monastery

However, Rafael's contribution to Spain's cause was not to be confined to the monastery. He, too, was called up by his country. Since the war was going on longer than at first expected, further recruits were mobilized, and among those drafted was Rafael. So on September 29, he left the monastery once again, and went to Burgos, where his family was staying, to join the army.[6]

Nonetheless, the illness that the Lord had wanted Rafael to have not only kept him from full monastic observance, it now made it impossible for him to do his duty for his country. All the medical examinations done by the army resulted in his being declared completely useless for and completely exempt from military service. No doubt it pained him to see his companions march off to the battlefront while he had to bear the disgrace of being useless for the service of his country.[7] But once more he accepted the will of God with resignation and contentment, while

6. Rafael, of course, was not the only monk to leave the monastery in order to serve his country. The community of San Isidoro generously offered more than thirty of its members as a contribution to the Nationalist cause, and they served in all the branches of the military, both at the various fronts and behind the lines.

7. Later, when Rafael was again declared unfit for military service during a new medical examination, he would remark that for the first time he regrets not serving God and Spain at the front.

showing kindness and a smiling countenance to all he dealt with, treating with great charity the sick and wounded, and ready to provide for the needs of those from his own monastery who had been mobilized with him, quite prepared to aid them in every way, even putting his car at their disposal.

Rafael was still with his parents during the month of October while he dealt with all the procedures he had to go through because of his uselessness for the army. Once again he was dressed in civvies, smoked and socialized with people in the outside world, far from his La Trappe. Still, amid the noise and movement and excitement in which he had to live, he did not forget to recollect himself interiorly in order to reflect on God's purpose in all that was happening around him.

Once the Nationalist forces had smashed through the siege of Oviedo, Rafael, together with his father and his brother Leopoldo, left Burgos for Oviedo in order to find out what remained of his family and his home in that city. Finding it impossible to reach the city, they went to Corruna to enter Asturias by way of Galicia. From there Rafael, glad to be able to render some useful service at least to his family, while unable to give any to the army, wrote a letter to his mother, telling her, "I am very glad to have come, for now that my uselessness prevents me from taking a rifle and serving my country, at least I am able at this point to be of use to Father."

Unable to enter Oviedo, they returned to Burgos, and from there Rafael went to Avila to visit his uncle and aunt before returning to the monastery. He enjoyed his stay with them and regarded it as a gift of God, but he kept experiencing such a strong attraction for La Trappe that he decided not to spend much time at Avila, and told his parents: "I do not want to spend much time here . . . After all, my La Trappe is my La Trappe . . . You understand?"

Entering for the third time

Burgos in wartime conditions—it was soon to become an important location for the Nationalist forces—did not seem the right place to live for various reasons, so Rafael's family moved to Villasandino, a village in the province where they owned various properties. Rafael's uncle and aunt, the Duke and Duchess of Maqueda, of whom he was so fond and with whom he shared such a particularly deep and intense spiritual relationship, accompanied them. All together they would be able to face the next few months, despite rather tenuous peace and the possibility of penury and privations. The presence of his uncle and aunt gave Rafael a good opportunity to continue by word his spiritual relationship with them, particularly as monastery usage had only allowed him to write them three letters (two to his uncle and one to his aunt) since returning to the monastery in January.[8]

Nonetheless, it seemed to Rafael that he had to return to La Trappe. For a third time he would renounce so much that was permissible in order to follow the persistent call of God, which included at that very time the risk of being found involved in religious life.[9] He cared nothing about the risk; he had to be faithful to the call he was convinced he had.

While his brother Fernando fought in the Nationalist army, as did many of the monks of his monastery, on December 6, 1936, Rafael, accompanied by his brother Leopoldo and his sister Mercedes, arrived at the monastery, and he entered the community for the third time, taking his post once again at his particular "combat" on behalf of Spain.

Rafael was well aware that his pen did not say what he wished because it did not know how. Nevertheless, once back in the monastery, two days after reentering, he began the booklet he entitled *My Copybook*; he was thinking of helping his brother Leopoldo, and also of helping himself in his solitude.[10]

8. In fact, between early January and late September, when he left the monastery for the army, all Rafael's letters, apart from the three to his uncle and aunt, amounted to four to his parents and one to his brother Fernando. During his stay outside, at this time, he wrote two more letters to his parents, from Corunna and Avila.

9. Between bishops, priests, and religious, thousands lost their lives, many of them cruelly murdered during the Civil War. Among them were eighteen Trappist monks of the abbey of Viaceli near Corunna. Rafael's father had written to him, in February of the same year, that he was concerned about the repercussions that the exceptional circumstances which obtained in Spain might have for the monks.

10. During this time, as far as is known Rafael wrote no letters, not even for Christmas. Of his booklet, Rafael says, "Some day, perhaps, my brother Leopoldo

During this stay in the monastery, Rafael has "bright days and cloudy days, calms and tempests"; he feels the burden of the Rule, the work, the silence, the lack of light on a sad, gray day of wind and cold, but he also experiences passing from desolation to consolation, when in our nothingness "we are no sooner immersed in temptation than we take wing, consoled by the least touch of God's love." Come what may, he keeps to his purpose, knowing well that, go where one may, one has ever the cross to carry, and nonetheless convinced that the cross is the only way to get to God.

The thought of God

It has been mentioned already that the thought of God permeates Rafael's writings. At this time it makes an even more emphatic appearance. He himself has assured us that he has acquired a feel for God that he lacked before, and that all his impressions of La Trappe have now been changed for him into one essential: God.

The God of Rafael is not only the infinite God who made the earth and humankind, the absolute Lord of all, who created all in an instant. He is not just the great God contemplated in creation; he is God whom one contemplates in the silence of one's heart; God whom we have within us, even if at times we seek him outside ourselves; God whose love is experienced with joy despite and in the midst of everything, and whose immense goodness makes Rafael reflect. God loves Rafael very much. From him he has received great gifts; he owes everything to him. He acknowledges in no uncertain way that God is the beginning, middle, and end of everything, and because of that is the motive for his living, the very reason for his existence. What Rafael experiences is God, what he suffers is for God, what he reflects on is God, what he

---

will read these lines." Further on he remarks that, in addition to his desire to help whoever reads his booklet to come close to God, he writes also in order to unburden himself: "My copybook! . . . I keep putting into it my intimate emotions . . . I do not care if no one ever reads it; nor do I care if someone laughs at the medley of ideas, the mixture of triviality and deep thoughts. No matter . . . I go on writing . . . It is an unburdening understood only by one who experiences it." [This booklet is the only available source that tells of his third stay in the monastery.—Trans.]

lives for is God. God is everything for him, God is in everything
and Rafael sees him in everything. He regards any time that is
not lived for God as time wasted, and believes it sheer futility to
be taken up with what is not God.

For Rafael, what is outside of God is nothing and should
be counted as nothing. God and God alone is the true way to
go. An interior voice tells him, "Expect nothing from the world
and from people . . . only God." He alone can fill our heart and
only he should fill our mind, and if he is not there, it is because
we are unwilling. Apart from him, there is nothing even in La
Trappe; God is what is most important in La Trappe. He alone is
permanent. "All the rest . . . is nothing; it comes and goes, and
as Saint Teresa says, 'Only God is fully satisfying; whoever has
God, lacks nothing.'"[11]

Having God, Rafael lacks nothing; God is his life and treasure,
that which no one can take away from him, not even by means
of war or law or shedding blood. It does not matter whether he
is happy or in disgrace; he is with God, and that is fully satisfying. He is happy with what he has; he does not look for anything
other than God, and he has God in the little cross of his illness.
His soul dilates when he experiences that God alone fills it: God,
the one thing necessary.

Since nothing disturbs the peace of one who longs for God
alone, Rafael is inclined to think that relative to God even the
Civil War is of no importance. While he really does grieve for
Spain, he remains in peace because even in the face of the mis-
fortunes of war, "God alone is fully satisfying."

So, convinced that there is only one sheer truth, God who
alone is permanent and unchangeable, and that all else disap-
pears in time, what goes on around him is not important for him
nor is the way that his life is developing:

> In the monastery, the days pass . . . What matter? It is only
> God and I. I still live on earth, surrounded by others . . . What
> does it matter? . . . there is only God and I . . . Looking at
> the present world I do not see greatness, I do not see wretch-
> edness, I do not see snow, I do not glimpse the sun . . . The

---

11. Here Rafael explicitly cites the poem mentioned in footnote 5 above.

world shrinks to a place . . . in that place there is a monastery,
and in the monastery . . . only God and I.

In the presence of God we must indulge neither in nostalgia
for the past nor in fear about the future. God is present and only
he is fully satisfying. "If we have Him now, what more is there to
desire? The desire to be united to His will is all one's heart hopes
for in this world, and this hope is tranquil, goes *with peace*, even
though not yet having sight of God is a gloomy grief." Seduced
by God, and as God's silent prisoner, Rafael finds that his heart
is groaning for the sight of God. He also experiences what Saint
Teresa calls "not living in myself" and "dying because I do not
die."[12] Still, he knows at the same time that the only proper behavior is to wait in the arms of God, who also waits for us, and
who will soon arrive. How much Rafael could have said about
God who loves him so much! But his pen is far too awkward an
instrument when it comes to speaking about God.

In greater solitude

The days go by and Christmas arrives, the first in all his life
that Rafael would spend away from his parents and home. He is
going to celebrate it in the monastery and rather differently, "with
more austerity and greater recollection," because "the Trappist at
this season does not want noise, he has no need of a worldly kind
of feast . . . The feast . . . he celebrates is in a heart in love with
Jesus, in joyous silence . . . with singing within . . . with love that
is quiet and mute," even if there "are moments at which the heart
remembers those it loves in the world outside, happy days in the
past . . . the warmth of home." But this does not embitter one
who offers his total poverty to God, his unencumbered heart; no,
with great understanding and fellow-feeling for others, he would
say that "feasting in the outside world with iced cakes and sweet
things is necessary . . . necessary also is silence for monks."

The New Year moves him to make some philosophical reflections about time, about the changeableness of things and of life
over against the unchangeableness of God. Rafael welcomes the

12. Poem 2 in Spanish text.

new year as a gift from God, and is indifferent to what it may bring him. All he wants is that the Lord help him to serve him better during it, for he has already wasted enough time. He lives waiting for death, like a child who dreams of waking up in the arms of God.

Shortly after Epiphany, Rafael had to keep to the Infirmary, cut off from the life of the community, deprived of the enjoyable company of his fellow monks at field work and in choir. His illness had grown worse at that time. Completely lacking in energy, weary, and suffering as well from hunger and great thirst, Rafael was forced to spend long hours in an armchair. At times he felt sad at seeing himself "in that condition in a monastery where one lives in continual penance," while his life goes by and his strength keeps gradually diminishing; but he knows how to make the most of his troubles, and he describes his sickness as a "blessing" because it makes him think of God and separates him from others. He thanks God for it, convinced that it is God's will for him, and for that reason he could speak of "living in order to fulfill our *purpose* as sick people." Besides, if God has sent him this cross, which weighs heavily on him at times, it is because of his special love for him, wanting him to be "as He is . . . nailed to the cross." He is so convinced that by loving the cross, all is gain, that he would not change places with the novice he was years ago. He finds that as he loves Christ more, the more trials Christ sends him, and he so gladly suffers for him that he discovers "what a great comfort it is to have a cross," and that there "is no better peace than that provided for him by suffering."

Rafael, who preferred the community living of La Trappe to the semi-eremitic life of the Carthusians because he needed "to see faces," was to spend a period of deep solitude in his cell in the Infirmary. God, who "is egotistic[13] and does not allow his friends to seek consolation apart from Him," meanwhile continued his work on the heart of Rafael, tearing up all that still holds him to earth and creatures. Deprived of the company of his fellow monks, detaching himself from creatures, Rafael would come

---

13. This expression "God is egotistic" was considered infelicitous by the second theologian-censor of Rafael's writings; at the same time, he indicates that in the context of the paragraph it appears nevertheless in a correct sense.

closer to God. At first the process causes him many tears, for "it really costs to ascend this little slope where one lets go of so many dreams, sometimes of affections, sometimes, it seems, of large pieces of one's very self" in order to reach those solitudes of soul and body to which the Lord wants to lead him. But later he discovers that total solitude is where one really meets God and where "one enjoys the colossal consolation of knowing oneself to belong *solely* to God." What a joy it is then "to be alone with God . . . what great peace we breathe when we find ourselves alone . . . only oneself and God!"

In the solitude in which he now lives, and which is part of the silence that pervades the monastery, and which makes possible all sorts of activities, Rafael spends his days reading books and translating, and reflecting on God and writing the copybook, which he would finish on February 6, 1937, the day before he left the monastery for the third time.

The third departure

Rafael had been able to make his cell his heaven on earth, and discovered that he was by no means alone in his solitude. Now he had to endure further purification and detachment. The Lord wanted to take away from him even the special solitude that at first cost him so much; and not only that but the whole environment that the monastery provided him with. What happened was another intensification of the illness[14] that in any case was taking its inevitable course. This made further medical examination necessary. Since the monastery could not provide the proper facilities, owing to the Civil War, the Abbot ordered him to return home once again until life in the monastery had returned to normal.[15]

---

14. In a letter to the novice master, Rafael will write later that he himself was responsible for this relapse, for not having taken care of his infirmity as he ought. (See below, p. 90).

15. We know that the Brother Infirmarian who attended Rafael was at the battlefront. Moreover, the life of the monastery was conditioned by the war: concretely, shortly after Rafael's departure some Italian military personnel in the service of Spain would be quartered there.

So, obedience obliged Rafael to leave his cell. Three times he thought he had left everything; moreover, he was convinced that he would die a Trappist. But on February 7, he left the monastery for the third time. The last words he wrote in his copybook before leaving make plain, on the one hand, his longing for the solitude that he is leaving and has acquired a taste for, and on the other hand, his welcoming of God's plan for him: "I was so content in my solitude! Fiat."

His interior disposition on leaving the monastery for the third time, when compared with those at his two previous departures, shows the change that has been wrought in Rafael. He himself discloses it in a careful examination of his dispositions:

> This is the third time that I lay aside the monastic habit . . . The first time I thought I would die, so upset was I . . . I thought that God had deserted me. The second time I left because of the war . . . I knew that returning to the monastery would cost me a lot . . . I saw that God was putting me to the test . . . The third time, this one . . . *so clearly do I see* God's hand, that it is all the same to me . . . Now I see neither that God deserts me nor that God puts me to the test . . . but that God loves me.[16]

---

16. This change of attitude between the second and the third departure from the monastery had come about in the space of four months. It seems right to think that it was speeded up by the experience of deep solitude that Rafael had lately been through in the Infirmary. In addition to this analysis of his interior, *My Copybook* gives two other significant analyses by Rafael: one about passing from a state of desolation to one of consolation on being touched interiorly by a light from God, found in a pleasant context of fun and games; and another that discerningly discusses the imperfection of seeking consolation apart from God in time of trial.

VII

WITH HIS FAMILY FOR THE LAST TIME

A new adjustment

On February 7, 1937, Rafael left the monastery for the third time. Under obedience he left all that goes with Trappist life. He particularly regretted having to leave the solitude which after quite some suffering had proved so fruitful, in order to return home to what it had cost him so much to leave. It seemed as if God took particular pleasure in dragging him from here to there and in asking him to renounce what he would later give back to him, or in giving him a liking for the solitude that he would later take away from him by sending him back to the outside world again. To live in peace through all of this demanded continual detachment and not a little psychological and spiritual adjustment from him to the different situations in which the Lord would have him live. Quite understandably, Rafael found himself somewhat bewildered at times by all the going and coming that the Lord had put him through in a few years, and that sometimes immersed him in a dark night of doubt about the renunciations he had made, about the direction of his life, about the three years of generous effort that seem like a meaningless giving into the hands of the God who misleads him. No doubt, by expressing his *Fiat* he surrendered himself into the hands of God, and when Rafael calmly considered all the marvels the Lord was ever doing for him, his bewilderment changed into an interior light that told him of the mercy of God. Nevertheless the "instability" to which the Lord subjected him continued to be a trial for Rafael, since stability is proper to the monastic life he was familiar with and desired.

He told the Assistant Novice Master of this in a letter:

> The Lord tries me greatly with this illness of mine that drags
> and brings me to and fro; and the spiritual effort involved be-
> cause of having no fixed abode, being no sooner in the outside
> world than back in the monastery, is something one has to
> experience if one is to understand it.

Rafael rejoined his family in Villasandino, where they still
were, owing to the impossibility of returning to Oviedo. His
uncle and aunt were there as well, which was undoubtedly a
consolation for Rafael just when he had to leave the monastery
once again. Now he had to rearrange his life in that corner of
Castile still unchanged despite the reverberations of the war.
He returned to the usual activities that gave him time for all he
wanted to do: walking in the fields, chatting amiably with the
servants and farmers, taking an interest even in his father's prop-
erty, making suggestions in matters concerning his family that
they accepted without hesitation, spending long periods in the
garden of the estate, spending time at music and at listening to
news of the war on the radio, joining in the family Rosary, Mass
and other religious practices.

Now he practiced virtue without affectation in the ordinari-
ness of daily life; in quiet and silent acceptance of his illness,
never complaining of it; in freely doing without food that he
liked; in going along with the preferences of others; in controlling
his lively and impatient temperament, showing kindness and
love to all in his family and overlooking whatever irked him;
and all this was the splendid result of that love for neighbor that
will be discussed soon further on. As was to be expected, Rafael
also returned to his canvasses and his paintbrushes. It can be said
that in God and in these instruments the monk and the artist that
he was took refuge. His most successful pieces come from this
time, and in all of them it seems as if God was guiding his hand,
giving his paintings a tone of deep religiousness.

Love triumphs in him

And yet Rafael now is not the same as he was before he
entered the monastery for the second time. Now he appears
more interiorly recollected, less exteriorly communicative. The

intensity of his love for God and neighbor has not lessened but has been transformed by the purification process he has been through. He was, perhaps, more sensitive before; now he is more single-minded, more guided by faith, but without being any less human, as he himself believes is the case. This may explain why it was not until March 18 that he wrote his first letter since leaving the monastery. He had decided not to write to anyone, being more than ever convinced that the more words one uses, the worse it is. He finds as well that he has become stupid when it comes to giving expression to what he really feels, just as the words themselves become stupid, trying to say something and unable to say anything. Even his aunt would later be surprised by his silence, although she was quite sure that Rafael's attitude towards her continued unchanged. When at last he broke his silence, he did so moved by charity towards his uncle who was going through a bad time.

Rafael often feels overwhelmed by the thought of "waiting," and he knows by experience "how pleasant waiting is for the one who waits . . . when it is Jesus who is going to arrive." He also knows "how pleasant it is to wait while doing good, while having a smile for both our brothers and our enemies." It is a case of being active while waiting. Although overwhelmed by the desire for God, and by the waiting, Rafael has also discovered the great treasure that consists in love for neighbor. This is why he writes to his uncle to encourage him, and why his advice to his aunt includes very definite rules about love for neighbor, when he invites her to be understanding and uncritical, and to make the lives of those around her pleasant, without dreading lest loving be a waste of time; being charitable, inoffensive, avoiding silences that at times can hurt more than the sharpest retorts. Starting out from acceptance of the way people really are, and that nothing except God is perfect, he goes so far as to invite her not only to be patient but to seek, as Jesus did, unsatisfactory people.[1] She was to love those who would, perhaps, despise her or misunderstand

1. Rafael writes to his aunt: "Jesus sought the company of the sick, the poor, and above all of sinners. He did not confine himself to the company of his friend Lazarus, whom he loved so much, but sought those who would cost him his blood, sought them at wedding festivities or in public places, gathering women who were sinners about him."

her, and also she must make sure not to disturb anyone by being inconsiderate to others in her immediate family under cover of performing her own devotions, because "excessive withdrawal can look like contempt, which is not what Jesus has taught us."[2] Not that all this should prevent her having her own times for silence and prayer, unbeknown to others.

As at other times, Rafael's advice reflects his own experience, for, thanks to the process of interior change that he has been through and to his own self-knowledge, he does not think that he has any right to make others change, but accepts them as they are. This he makes plain in a rapid survey of what he has been through:

> Solitude was necessary. It was necessary to renounce my own will. Illness was and is necessary. For what? Well, look, while the Lord has been bringing me to and fro, without a fixed abode, teaching me what I really *am*, and detaching me from creatures, at times gently, at times with rough blows—through all that journey, which I can see so clearly, I have learned one thing, and my mentality has undergone a change . . . I have learned to love people *as they are* and not as I would wish they were . . .[3]

The transformation that has been wrought in him, and which, for want of a better term, he calls "serenity," makes it possible for him to overlook the way people become uncouth because of the rough treatment of the world; not only that, he finds himself open to them, with the attitude of one who, after putting creatures aside in order to go to God unhindered, returns to them without fear, once firmly rooted in him whose presence fills his heart, wishing to share his own experience with them. Rafael says it this way:

2. Admittedly, while he counsels his aunt in this way, he himself would spend his mornings completely alone, but his place in his family differed from hers in her family.

3. What with all the writing on psychology, on group dynamics, on interpersonal relationships, etc., Rafael's idea of accepting people as they are may perhaps not surprise us nor may we value it properly; yet he has arrived at this conclusion through personal conviction, thanks to self-knowledge and above all the example of Jesus who welcomed all with all their weaknesses.

One loves people instead of dreading to approach them, and one seeks them out as well, in order to teach them the wisdom that Christ has taught us—charity . . . How much I would like to share (the state of my soul) with the whole world, and that the whole world should be madly in love with God and think of nothing else, and that the whole world were as happy as I am, who have nothing, not even health, and have everything . . . all that can be had in this life; I have God deep in my heart, and I desire nothing; believe me, one who has full happiness.

Happy in God

Rafael at this time is absolutely happy; not with a facile happiness, but with one that comes from not desiring anything for himself. He takes as the sovereign and sublime rule of his life the program of "deny yourself, take up your cross every day and follow me." He lives with the "gladness of one who lives for God alone, of one who trusts in God alone, of one who hopes in God alone," experiencing in his own being "how great is the gladness of living when one has God and God alone." Having him, all "the problems that life brings us" are cut down to size, "problems the solution of which is found in . . . God alone."

He himself has found in God the solution for his suffering. The cross costs him more and more; it burdens him more and more; but the "God alone," who fills him more and more, gives him strength. He has discovered that the Lord who leads him with loving care places him beside the cross and invites him not to despise it and not to weep because of the route that the Lord plans for him. For one should not weep over one's own crosses, but only for not loving Jesus, for "not loving sufficiently." This is why Rafael has made his cross his only treasure, well aware that it brings him closer to the Lord, who by his love strengthens him when weak. As he says:

> How great is the intimacy of Jesus with those who weep! How blest are the tears, pains, and sickness that are our treasure, the only thing we have, what enables us to come close to Jesus, since the little love we have for him is so soft and weak that by itself it is not enough!

And so, happy with God, with the treasure that his cross is, Rafael lives at Villasandino, convinced that everything in his life is an occasion for becoming better. He himself mentions how he would spend his time when at home at this period: "I spend the mornings completely alone and given over to the Sacred Scriptures, in which I continually find the inexhaustible mine of the word of God." Having experienced the richness of solitude and silence, which give rest to the mind and are the indispensable condition for prayer, he has decided to include them in his life at home, a decision his family no doubt agreed to. Nonetheless, his present situation, which possibly is not altogether helpful as regards solitude and silence, has helped him to deepen both of them by giving them a more spiritual meaning. So he understands solitude as "the absence of desire for anything that comes from creatures . . . no matter what our surroundings; keeping one's heart free and detached from everything"; and he understands silence not only as silence in word and deed, but something much deeper that not even thinking dares disturb, very difficult to explain, but without which one cannot live.[4]

At the end of April or early May, Rafael went southwest to bring his grandmother Fernanda and his aunt María, the Duchess of Maqueda, who had both spent some months at Villasandino, to Toro. On the way back, he stopped at his La Trappe, and found it rather noisy because of the one thousand Italian troops lodged at the monastery on account of the Civil War. Only the Father Master was available for a moment; Rafael attended the chanting of Vespers.

Back with his family, the months go by while Rafael lives in the pleasant and serene gladness of one who really surrenders himself into God's hands, in a "silence to all that is exterior, *despite* being completely immersed in the outside world." He lives waiting and hoping, but with the great serenity that he both lives and recommends. The serenity that is able to discover God's love on the path of self-sacrifice and renunciation, and that is present even in "the wanting and hoping of one who, possessing nothing, expects

---

4. These ideas of Rafael's resemble Hesychast spirituality, which demands not just exterior solitude and silence but attaining to interior tranquility through the absence of all reasonable and unreasonable concern.

everything," frequently shows itself in the Rafael of this period. Having grasped the reason for living, and that living is for God and for him alone, nothing in the world can now disturb Rafael, not even having to live through the insignificance of being nothing and of no use; God alone is his desire. And if it can become difficult to be useless while others carry on the war, to be a sick and useless oblate in a monastery during a war, "God above all . . . May his will be fully done." This is where one really is in settled peace, in serenity, free from one's own wishes that can so subtly invade the desire for God, as Rafael himself says with such precision:

> How pleasant it is to wait while thinking of God! . . . But the waiting stretches out painfully once other desires that are not from God afflict us; when our selfishness refuses the cross; when the longing for God is *infected even if ever so subtly* by loathing for living. How often we deceive ourselves by thinking that it is God when it is not, and I prefer not to be dogmatic about what perfection is! God, keep me free from that! Still, I do believe that the longing to see God and the impatience of waiting are made perfect by total submission to his will, by the serenity of one who desires nothing.

Viewing things this way, Rafael is not bothered in any way by the medical examination that awaits him. Knowing that we must seek neither repose nor rest in this life, he is not bothered by his illness. Intent on loving Jesus intensely, he has no time to busy himself with his health, with his crosses or with his consolation. What God may want from him, that shall be.

Three "spiritual" letters to his uncle

On September 25 and 26, Rafael writes two letters to his uncle. He writes because he writes. Or better, he writes in order to share what goes on within him, his interior living of the "God alone" that seems too much for him to keep in, and to which he wants to give free rein with someone who understands him. He tells him this at the beginning of the first of the two letters this way:

> Dear brother, I do not know why with pen in hand I have begun to write . . . Really, I do not know; there is no need and

I have nothing to say. There is only a reason, although very slight, and that reason is the desire I have—I have it still—the desire to talk about Him . . . I tell you all this . . . because only one who loves God a little can grasp it.

And Rafael has in all truth attained his objective. In two of the letters, he mentions God at least 84 times, and 22 of these are in the "God alone" form mentioned already, and that by now has become a predominant idea for him. For, after all, what is there outside of God? Outside of God there is nothing, and "neither the heart nor the soul finds rest outside of God; people have nothing to say to you; you find nothing in books." It is God who fills one with love and at the same time helps us to wait in hope. "How is it possible to talk to people when one's heart and soul are full of love for God? It is a miracle from God that he steals one's soul and still lets one live on earth." Love for the Lord prevents both pain and pleasure from troubling one's peace of soul, and even waiting becomes pleasant. "God alone! How pleasant it is to live this way!"

Rafael knows well that the world, so calculating, prudent, and sensible, so set on being reasonable, does not think like that. Unconcerned about arguing with it, he goes on with the "blest madness that enables us to live free from fondness for the earthly," being convinced besides that "there is more foolishness and folly in a worldly-wise person than in a million souls crazy about Christ," among whom he counts himself. Clearly perceiving the futility of everything here, thus does Rafael live, thinking of heaven and waiting in hope; waiting with the help of Mary.

On October 11, Rafael writes to his uncle what could be called his "Marian letter." He tells him clearly that he wants to send him a few words and spread himself a little talking about the Lady, still remembering the Marian ambience of the monastery, where the Virgin "lovingly smiles when some insignificant brother weeps." Rafael would have liked to fill reams and reams, chanting the beauties of Mary, and he regrets not having the words and the heart of David to do it. He thinks that, though a prophet, David knew nothing of the Virgin, otherwise he doubtless would have uttered some lovely things about her. He who said, "In God alone have I hoped," had he known the most holy Virgin, would have added, "and that hope is Mary." She is really a gift of God to us, a great mercy of God for people. Consequently, Rafael believes "that there is no danger of loving Mary too much . . . because all that we entrust to the Lady, Jesus receives with increase . . . that loving Mary, we love God, and that *it takes nothing from Him*, but does altogether the opposite." This is why he cannot understand "how it is possible to live without loving Mary."

Preparing for his last return

Towards the end of October, Rafael goes to Burgos for another medical examination in connection with the army, and stays there three days for that purpose. With 42/1000 of sugar in the urine, he is once again declared totally useless. His reaction now to his uselessness for military service is not what it was the first time. Rafael now lives far more serenely, surrendered into God's hands. He himself mentions it in a letter to Brother Tescelino, his one-time Infirmarian,[5] who is also away from the monastery because of the war. He tells the Brother:

> The first time I was declared useless, as you well know, I felt quite fed-up at not being fit to serve God and Spain at the battle-front . . . and perhaps firing a shot or two . . . Now, believe me, it is all the same to me, for I have adverted to the fact that what I may desire is worthless in God's sight, and that the best thing to do is to put oneself in God's hands and leave it at that. May he do with me and *with you* what he likes: do you not agree?

So they send Rafael from Saint Joseph's hospital to his home, and there he is "waiting for . . . *I know not what.*" For his part, he has already written to the Abbot telling him that, once the medical examination is done, he will return to the monastery. Because of his ill health, Rafael has been certified as unfit for military service in the war; he is also "useless" for soldiering under the Rule of Saint Benedict since he is unable to observe it fully. But he continues in his determination, despite all indications to the

---

5. Rafael enjoyed an affectionate and deep friendship with this Brother, as his letters to him show, and as does a letter to his aunt where he mentions him.

contrary, to reenter the monastery, with all the embarrassing exceptions it will bring him. It is for the Superiors to decide about and confirm once more what Rafael believes to be an interior call to live in his La Trappe.

The Novice Master, Father José Olmedo, replies, telling him that he may return whenever he likes, for the doors of the monastery are always open to him; however, he should think it over carefully and at leisure, for now they have no Infirmarian and it would be a pity if what happened to him before were to recur. Rafael understands that this reply "*humanly* speaking is very prudent," but he views the matter differently, as he says when unburdening himself to Brother Tescelino, the only person he writes to at this time, for their mutual encouragement:

> Suppose that you are at home sick, well cared for and attended to, almost a cripple, useless . . . , in a word, unable to do a thing for yourself. But if one day you were to see through your window Jesus going by . . . If you were to see that Jesus was being followed by a crowd of sinners, the poor, the sick, the lepers. If you were to notice that Jesus was calling you and was for *giving* you a place among those who follow him, and looked at you with those divine eyes that radiate love, tenderness, forgiveness, and were to say to you, "Why do you not follow me?" . . . What would you do? Would you by any chance reply to him . . . , "Lord, I would follow you if you were to give me an Infirmarian . . . If you enabled me to follow you *comfortably* and without danger to my health . . . I would follow you if I were in good health and strong enough to fend for myself . . . ?" No, rather . . . without considering your needs . . . you would prefer to say to him, "I am coming, Lord; I care nothing about my ailments, nor about death nor about eating nor about sleeping . . . If you allow me, I am coming."

Without considering his condition or what might happen to him in the future, giving no thought to himself, caring nothing that the course he will take would prove difficult, ridding himself of all human fear, Rafael is ready to reenter the monastery. Deep within himself he is aware of the "loving look of Jesus" who says to him, "*You may come when you like* . . . Do not mind if you are the last; do I love you any the less because of that? Maybe I love you more!" And although he is aware as well that "the flesh draws" and that the world calls him a crazy fool, he knows that nothing can compare with the call of the Lord and "not even suffering until the end of the world is worth the loss incurred by neglecting to follow Jesus." His only desire is to love God; what he wants is to serve him. He sees his La Trappe, he sees a cross, and he heads in that direction, so avid is he to leave a life of comfort. That is the whole thing. He will love as far as he is able, be it much or little, "but in the house of God and in silence." Anything else is not to follow his vocation—his vocation as a Trappist oblate, as one who obeys although without vows. That, to him, does not matter. This sick and useless oblate is happy because "his only desire is to love God and to occupy some corner or other in a Cistercian Trappist monastery," clothed only in the habit that is the cross of Christ, and following only the rule that is the will of God.

Although Rafael's parents think that he will spend the winter with them, he is thinking of setting out for his La Trappe very soon, once he has spent a few days with his brother Fernando, who is returning to the battlefront. Once more it will cost him much to leave his family, but he will do it, since "lovers of Jesus are not held back by love for parents or siblings." It is true that the thought of returning to the monastery makes him suffer greatly, for he knows where he is going and what he is facing; but he trusts Mary very much; she has always helped him. And so, the total solitude that will soon be his, the lack of normal creature comfort and perhaps the lack of understanding, do not frighten or discourage him; rather, they do the very opposite, since he hopes that all that he may encounter will help him to experience the loveliness of "having nothing except God."

On November 29, Rafael writes to the Father Master to tell him that, unless he receives some indication to the contrary, he will reenter the monastery sometime after the [feast of the] Immaculate [Conception], being as yet unable to fix the exact date. In any case, he wants to spend Christmas, the family feast, away from his own home, offering this sacrifice to the Lord, and thus associate himself with so many of his fellows, who, because of the war, find themselves away from home. Rafael does not want to be less absent. Besides, he has been staying with his brother Fernando, who has already rejoined those at the battlefront, and he ought to set off for his battlefront at his La Trappe in order to help Fernando at his own.

Rafael uses this letter to the Father Master to dispel any anxiety the latter might have because of the lack of an Infirmarian at the monastery. He tells him that that is not a reason for not reentering, particularly since he himself was responsible for his relapse that last time. His self-love, his desire to do what he could not and should not do, his not humbling himself because of his illness, his being fickle and disobedient, his "not seeing that that [being sick] is the way the Lord wants him to be," brought on his relapse. By now he has changed greatly; he hopes to be much better and more obedient, in every way obedient and humbling himself before the community, watching over his illness as if it were his most valuable treasure, and for which gift he thanks the Lord, since it helps him to place himself in God's hands. He hopes to be able to administer the doses of insulin to himself and to tell the Brother in charge exactly the diet he needs to keep to; he hopes also to avoid all bashfulness, even to the extent of being ready to ask for and eat meat in the middle of the Chapter if he needs it. All this is very difficult, but it does not amount to much because "it will be of short duration."[6] In addition, Rafael has "come to realize that real mortification consists in doing what you neither like nor desire, even if your desires seem to you to be holy and good," remembering that "Christ taught us to suffer, taught us to keep silent, taught us not to desire anything other than what the Father might want."

The days that keep him from his La Trappe seem rather long to Rafael. He claims he does not know how to live in the outside world, breathing its air laboriously, suffering "badly" from divine love and longing for eternal life, and desiring to be crazy, "crazy about Christ," and so needing the seclusion of his La Trappe. Rafael's only ambition in this life is to live in the house of God, living hidden away in it and taking the last place.

Still, despite such desires, Rafael considers himself a weakling and worthless, in need of the help of everything and of every-

---

6. Already in January of that year, just before leaving the monastery for the third time, he was convinced that he would not live long. He wrote at that time, "Here . . . is one . . . [who] knows . . . that in a very little time all will end."

one, and so in a friendly way he asks for prayers on his behalf from Brother Tescelino and from Father Francisco. To the latter he writes:

> Please do not forget to commend me sometime to Her [the Holy Virgin] during Mass, and mention it also to the Novices that in their prayers they may remember their brother Rafael . . . Believe me, I need it. The outside world is so hard to shake off! Family! Liberty! . . . Still . . . believe me, Father Francisco, I would leave it all once, twice, thrice, a thousand times for Jesus; but I will always need help from heaven, for I am one, and you know it, who is weak and very attached to everything.

This "leave it all . . . a thousand times" he had already used before entering the monastery for the second time. And it seems right to consider it to be true in his case, since he has done it for a third time, and is ready to do it for a fourth, even if he has to break his heart to do so.

VIII

TO DIE AT HIS LA TRAPPE

The final reentry

From the time of Rafael's first departure from the monastery, the Lord had been giving him an understanding that the outside world was not where he wanted him to be and that he wanted him close to the sanctuary. On December 14, 1937, Rafael told his mother that once again the time had come to go "to the house of the Lord." He himself would later say, "I return to my La Trappe in order to continue fulfilling my vocation, which simply consists in loving God in self-sacrifice and self-renunciation, without any other rule than blind obedience to his divine will." He believed that he was "fulfilling it *today* by obeying, without vows and as an oblate, the superiors of the Cistercian abbey of San Isidoro de Dueñas."

Although Rafael's announcement seemed premature to his mother, he added quite decisively, "Tomorrow I shall return to my La Trappe," which was quite feasible since there was no need for special luggage or arrangements. Years before, Rafael had been more or less whimsical and fickle; by now he had renounced everything and owned nothing. Even his canvasses, his drawings and paintings of Jesus would remain at his home.

At 11 in the morning of December 15, Rafael left home once again. The farewell was quiet, simple, painful. Both he and his mother knew that this was their final good-bye on earth. It was a kind of death, worse perhaps than death itself. Rafael himself wrote of it the following day:

> Yesterday, leaving my home and my parents and my brothers and sister, was one of the days of my life on which I suffered

most. This is the third time that I have left all to follow Jesus,[1] and I think that this time it was a miracle of God, for it is quite certain that by my own efforts I could not have come to the Infirmary of my La Trappe to endure sufferings such as hunger in body, due to my illness, and solitude of heart, since I feel that people are far away. God alone . . . God alone . . . God alone. That is my motto . . . that is my only thought.

Rafael knows very well what he is returning to at the monastery. There he had lived as one of the sick in the solitude of the Infirmary, and it had been at the price of no few tears. As he leaves home now, all that experience of suffering comes to his mind, making his heart tremble, and he has to respond to it. He does so by fully accepting the fact that in knowingly going to his La Trappe he is shortening his life span, and that there he will experience far more acutely the burden of his incurable illness than he would have at home where everything is at his service. Later he would mention all of this without ambiguity: "When I left home, I left with *deliberate* intent a whole series of remedies that my illness requires, and I came in order to embrace a lifestyle that makes it impossible to take proper care of so sensitive an illness. I knew perfectly well what I was coming to."

His state of mind in view of such great suffering helps one to understand an incident that his brother Leopoldo mentioned when he was a witness at the Process of Palencia. He said:

> I went with him to his La Trappe when he returned there for the last time. We left Villasandino in a car which the Servant of God drove. When the monastery came into view, some 500 meters away from it, he stopped the car, gave me the wheel, and asked me for a cigarette. Suddenly I noticed that he was weeping. Then I asked him what was wrong with him. He pointed to the monastery and said to me, "Look at that: a subsidiary of

---

1. In fact, it was not the third but the fourth time that Rafael left his family and all else in order to enter the monastery. If he thought it was the third time, he must have done so from forgetfulness or because he takes no account of his short stay with his family from September 29 to December 6, 1936, when he left the monastery because of the Civil War. Still, even this brief stay at home demanded a further renunciation on reentering the monastery, as already described.

hell." Gradually he calmed down, we continued our trip, and he
stayed in the monastery once again.

How can we explain the strong terms, "Look at that: a sub-
sidiary of hell?" In no way can they be understood as implying
the absence of God, whom Rafael had already experienced in
suffering itself. Rather, they refer to the place where he has suffered and expects to suffer yet again. And surely it is not the
suffering that might come to him from the community but from
his illness itself, which among other inconveniences makes him
feel an almost constant, intense hunger and thirst, and above all
the psychological solitude so strongly experienced, owing to his
being confined more or less continually to the Infirmary.[2] Any-
how, the monastery seemed to Rafael at that moment a place of
great suffering, so that his firm decision to reenter it is this time a
sign of the heroism of his fortitude in bearing physical pain and
dryness of spirit. He had good reason to say to the Lord a few
days after reentering:

I have left my home . . . I have shattered my heart piece by
piece . . . I have emptied my soul of worldly desires . . . I
have embraced your cross. What are you waiting for, Lord? If
what you desire is my solitude, my sufferings, and my being
desolate . . . Take it all, Lord; I ask nothing of you.

"God and my soul": motives and longings

Once back in the monastery, Rafael tells of his being welcomed
once again with kindness beyond his deserving. Nonetheless, another trial awaited him, in addition to the ones he had already fore-
seen: not having the spiritual director he had had in the monastery
until then. This would make still greater the solitude in which he
was to spend the last months of his life. It was one of those trials

2. Although in a letter of December 1 Rafael asserts to the infirmarian that,
in addition to absolute solitude and lack of human consolation, misunderstanding may also await him, we know that in general the community appreciated
Brother Rafael. But we also know that in the infirmary he had for table compan-
ion a mentally ill brother, secluded in the infirmary, who mortified him by telling him that "he had come to eat the bread of the poor." Thirty years later, a little
before his death, this sick brother was full of eulogies for Brother Rafael.

that God allows to befall his chosen ones, and it happened this way. At a time when it was least expected the Abbot changed the confessors appointed for the novices. Owing to Church law then in force, Rafael could no longer go for confession or direction to his former confessor, but would have to avail himself of another, less able to provide direction to one of his spiritual stature.

This event, undoubtedly providential for Rafael, was so for us as well, since his former director, during his last session with him, got the great idea of ordering him to write about all that was happening in his interior life, with a view to enabling him to give him guidance at the first opportunity that might present itself. Rafael, who wanted to obey in all matters, began on December 16 to record in an ordinary copybook all that was going on in his soul. Thinking only of writing for his confessor and director, Rafael records his good as well as his bad thoughts, the temptations that assail him, the longings of his heart and the immeasurable love that fills his soul. These pages are a kind of holy relic of the spirit that enlivened Rafael in this final stage of his life. In fact they are the principal source for our knowledge of him, since apart from them we have only four letters, which he wrote to his family and to the former Infirmarian, who was outside the monastery because of the war.

The first day that Rafael began these writings (which he entitles *God and my soul: Conscience Notes,* adding the word *Private*) he mentions the motives that have persuaded him to enter the monastery this time. The first of them is very important, and contributes to a better understanding of the persistent desire that Rafael had to reenter his La Trappe despite outward indications —above all his illness—that would seem to exclude him from the monastic life whose regulations he was unable to observe fully. He experiences in his heart a further rule, a further calling, that of loving God in the cross and in self-sacrifice, and he believes that he can achieve it best in the monastery. Thus he writes:

I have come for various motives:

1. Because I think that in the monastery I can better fulfill my vocation to love God in the cross and in self-sacrifice,

2. Because Spain is at war and to help my fellow believers in the fight,

3. In order to make good use of the time that God may give me and to hasten to learn to love the cross.

Intent on eternity, Rafael wants to make good use of what remains of his lifetime, which he senses is not much. And he wants to make better use of it in the monastery by learning in practice the wisdom of the cross, which in fact would prove a notable feature at this period of his monastic life. But he wants this not only for his own benefit: he would include it in the apostolic dimension he already has (as has been mentioned), which now focuses his attention on the Civil War raging in Spain, and on helping his side in the fight.[3]

Together with these motives, Rafael is clear about his intent in the monastery, in the life that, for the last time, he sets out to live there:

My only intent in the monastery is:
1. To unite myself absolutely and totally to the will of Jesus,
2. To live only for love and suffering,
3. To be the last and least, except for when it comes to *obeying*.

United to the will of God

Rafael's intent is to unite himself absolutely to the will of God, because "wanting only what God wants is the logical thing for one who is really his lover," and he has come to the monastery precisely in order to realize more fully his vocation to love God. For this reason alone he ardently longs to carry through what God wants from him, while at the very same time he experiences the gladness of being freed from the burden of his self-will. He wants to do everything for God's sake, his only rule being God's will.

3. Later on Rafael would explain more fully the apostolic motivation behind his vocation when he wrote: "*My vocation is to suffer*; to suffer in silence for the whole world; to sacrifice myself together with Jesus for the sins of those brothers of mine, priests and missionaries: for the needs of the Church, for the sins of the world, the needs of my family, which I want to see not in earthly plenty but closely united to God."

Having no desire apart from God, all he wants is that his life be a constant *consent* to God's will.

Given an interior disposition of this kind, it is easy to understand that he is indifferent to everything and complains of nothing. He sees that God's will for him is that he should not take vows nor observe the Rule fully. God has given him an incurable illness, but he does not care, since it does not prevent him from loving God, and little by little he has grown used to always doing what he neither wants to do nor likes to do.

Wanting to fulfill God's will to the end and understanding it as a dynamic reality, he asks the Lord to make it clear to him and to give him a humble spirit to perceive it and fulfill it, and not allow him to reject his divine suggestions. He certainly does find God's will even in the little and least that happens to him, and he believes besides that he should fulfill it by humble obedience. He has experienced the great gladness of living without self-will, and so true is it that he has a measureless desire to fulfill only God's will, that whenever he remembers, he makes an act of conformity with the divine will. And he experiences such union with it that even when he suffers, once he realizes that God wants it that way, he suffers no longer. He is so attached to God's will that it is clear to him that he is unable to do anything that God does not want, and so he achieves his desire of adoring the will of God that he has made his own.

This identification with God's will has transformed Rafael's mentality; he wants only what God wants because apart from God's desires, our desires are worthless; all that we might desire that God does not desire is sheer futility. Consequently, he does not want any freedom that will not bring him to God, nor does he want consolation or gladness or pleasure. Why, where at times in the past he would have liked to fly away to God because he knows that God is awaiting him, he now no longer has any desire to die.

Rafael has attained such a level of indifference that he is in no way concerned about what the new year of 1938 may bring him; he neither knows nor cares. He belongs to God, and God may do whatever he likes with him. Nothing matters for him now. It does not matter that he has to live walled in, unable to see the sunsets; neither his life nor his health nor his illness matter to him now; creatures do not matter to him now, nor do people's defects distress him. What used to make him suffer makes no difference to him now; what would humiliate him once, now makes him laugh. His insignificance in the monastery as an oblate does not matter to him now. He finds his only consolation in doing God's will. He wants nothing but God. Once he did not know what it was that he was thirsting for, but the Lord has enabled him to understand: what he longs for is God. At the same time, Rafael, for his part, senses that he himself is a being possessed by God.

In his desire to live and die a Trappist, Rafael once longed for a corner at La Trappe; now even this no longer matters to him. Thanks to his lived experience, he has come to grasp the futility of everything, the futility of loving what perishes. Everything is changing in his soul; what God is doing within it is so wonderful! His very indifference is nothing less than one of the transformations that God has wrought in it: Rafael asked the Lord for that virtue, and he has granted it to him. By now, nothing external affects him as he centers his life more and more on God: "Only you, Lord . . . ! Only you!" On rising he utters his "God alone is fully satisfying," and he repeats it when he lies down, asking nothing from the Lord, wanting only to love him and fulfill his will.

To reach such a spiritual disposition, to part with everything before death, Rafael admits, costs a bit, but afterwards "how well one lives without a thing and only in God's hands!" Moreover, he considers that there is no merit in desiring nothing once one is in love with God, since nothing could be more in the nature of things. All he wants is to love madly, wanting his life in the year that is beginning to be "guided solely by love for Jesus . . . by a love both very great and very pure."

To live loving

The dream that Rafael has brought with him to the monastery of living only for loving is rooted in him at one and the same time both naturally and supernaturally. He wants only to love because he is a man made for loving, and because he has come to realize that all that the Lord wants from him is his love fully detached from everything and everyone.[4] Because of this, on the first day of 1938, Rafael has decided to make a vow to always love the Lord. He mentions it as follows:

> During prayer this morning I made a vow. I have made the *vow to always love* Jesus. I have come to realize what my vocation is. I am not a religious . . . nor am I a lay person . . . I am nothing . . . Blest be God, I am only someone in love with Christ. He wants nothing except my love, and wants it detached from everything and everyone . . . To love Jesus in all, through all and always . . . Love alone. Humble, generous, unattached, sacrificial love, in silence . . . May my life be nothing more than an act of love.[5]

And since he wants his life to be solely an act of love and his only wish is to love Jesus madly, Rafael would prefer to cease living were he able to live without loving him. And when he experiences the meagerness of his love, the anguish of wanting to love and not being able to, he would prefer to die of love, since he is unable to live solely of love. It does not matter to him whether he dies or lives; only what the Lord wills. Rafael would prefer to either die or live, provided it meant doing something for love of the Lord. He would go further and would like love to be the cause of his death; he would like to die of love, considering that love is stronger than death itself, and acquires by its means an eternal duration: "What a beautiful profession I am going to

---

4. This *necessity* which Rafael perceives with regard to love had already been revealed in his writing of two years earlier, where it appeared as a consequence of God's design for him, a design perceived now in continuity. Cf. pp. 57–59.

5. Since he was permanently prevented, because of his illness, from taking the vows of a religious that could have helped him grow in love for God and neighbor, Rafael wanted with this vow of always loving Jesus to fix himself once and for all, and directly, on love. Although it might seem strange that Rafael never mentions this vow expressly again, he does insist on its content, as when on January 31 he writes again, "I would like my life to be one sole act of love." Love, in fact, fills his whole life. He says, "I wish my poor and sickly life were a flame in which, through love, were consumed . . . all the sacrifices, all the pains, all the renunciations, all the solitudes." Rafael has no further need of mentioning his vow of love; he lives it, and that for him is enough.

make the day of my death! . . . Eternal vows of love! . . . For
ever . . . for ever . . . "

His present situation is one of nonobservance [of monastic
rules]; meanwhile, his life of love will be his rule, his vow, his only
reason for existing. Knowing that, apart from loving and serving
Christ, all else is nothing, all he wants is to love God, and he does
it within himself. It does not depend on being clothed in brown
or in white, with or without a cowl.[6] Rafael is quite certain that
only love for God can satisfy the soul. It is precisely love that is
the answer to the questions with which his special situation in
the monastery presents him, questions that represent a crisis for
his monastic identity. He writes:

> I live a life of ease, comfortable and unmortified . . . the result
> being that I am neither a lay person, since I live in a religious
> house, nor am I a religious, since I live like a lay person . . .
> My God, what then am I? . . . I do not know, and at times,
> when I think of it, it seems to me that I do not care what I am
> . . . But what can I do? Useless and sick . . . Poor Brother Ra-
> fael! Enough for you to purify your intention *at every moment*,
> and *at every moment* to love God; to do everything for love
> and with love . . . The deed in itself is nothing and worthless.
> What counts is the way it is done.

Rafael is not a religious; he considers himself to be nothing
and a nobody; he is the last of all; but he would like nonetheless
to love God as he loves no one else. For this he has come to the
monastery, to learn the unique wisdom of love. And he is learning it at the price of much suffering.

To live suffering

The dream Rafael had on entering the monastery, of living
only to love and to suffer, he keeps on making real in its duality
at this period of his life, being convinced that the more he suffers,
the more he will love the Lord and the happier he will be. He so
much wants to offer to God the love that God asks of him. He
knows how to accept suffering, believing that what is suffered

---

6. The essential monastic over-garment.—Trans.

for the sake of love will be of some benefit to him, and he asks himself what use his life in his La Trappe would be if he did not suffer, having come there to suffer.

In fact, from the moment he reenters the monastery, he does not lack suffering. The very first day of his final stay there, his copybook reports that he is suffering greatly, and a few days later, in connection with Christmas, it does so again when mentioning his deep grief. It reports similarly later on, only a month before his death:

> I suffer greatly . . . yes. At times the load I have taken on my weak and sickly shoulders is very great . . . I look back, and . . . it is so hard for one who had everything and lacked nothing to live in poverty . . . ! I look ahead . . . and the slope I have to climb seems so steep . . . ! At times Jesus hides himself so thoroughly! My life has shrunken to a form of *continual self-renunciation in everything.* And that is not easy for a creature so frail and fragile as I am . . . That is why I suffer.

Rafael would not dare to pray for sufferings and the cross, since, given his weakness, it would seem to him proud presumption. But he has in his own person a sure source of suffering: his illness, which, in addition to the physical effects it might have on him, places him in a situation and a special solitude in the monastery that constitute another source of suffering.

No doubt, as the days and years go by, Rafael realizes more and more that the great mercy of God in his regard consists in the illness he has sent him, which is still his great treasure, but which nonetheless does not cease to be a heavy burden that God has laid on him.

There was a slight respite in the progress of his illness, which Rafael made use of to assuage his father's understandable anxiety. On February 14 he writes that he has never been in better health, even if he still takes doses of insulin, and that he has put on quite some weight, and is being treated much too well and very charitably. Still, just four days later, writing in his copybook, he makes evident the great suffering his illness brings him, the severe symptoms that he now experiences. Before returning to the monastery Rafael had never known what it was to cry because of the pangs of hunger. Now he sheds tears because of the hunger that is one of the symptoms of his diabetes, hunger that is hardly ever satisfied in the monastery. This is indeed mortification, unlike his first Lent in his La Trappe, the fasting of which now seems a joke to him. His life now is a continual Lent. Many a day he has to leave the refectory in tears, crying at times after the evening collation, suffering greatly in body and morale. But he is able to bless God when he finds himself more fervent and closer to God, the more hunger he suffers and the more his legs give way under him. He also blesses the new Infirmarian, who neither knows about nor understands his illness, who has no idea as to the hunger he has and how much it makes him suffer![7] True, at times he felt unable to cope with the suffering that hunger and solitude and silence brought him, but he never failed to experience the help he asked of God in prayer.

Nor did Rafael shed tears only because of the hunger and bodily weariness resulting from his illness; he shed them also because of the solitude it placed him in by obliging him to live in the Infirmary, thus preventing him to a great extent from sharing in the balance of community living. At Christmas time, for example, he mentions being in a vast solitude. No doubt, in the seclusion of his Infirmary cell, he reflected on the goodness of God, who had brought him to religious life, and now speaks to him in the silence of his heart. But feeling so lonely in his La Trappe brought him many a tear because of the strong temptation that at times accompanied it. Sometimes the physical and spiritual isolation in which he finds himself, having no one to alleviate his situation, to speak to his heart and encourage him, seems grievous to him. He suffers from bodily and spiritual need, and besides, God hides himself from him and leaves him all alone with the cross. So strong at certain moments are the boredom the solitary life inflicts on him, the gloom that envelops him, and the lack of a guide with whom to share the pain in his heart, that he goes so far as to say that his coming to the monastery was a piece of self-deception.

7. During the last months of his life, Rafael was under the care of Brother Domingo, who gave him only the same amount of food as was given to others of the sick. Witnesses during the Process agreed that Rafael had to endure many privations at this time because of the way the Infirmarian treated him; some even claimed that he gave him less food than was allowed. Still, they asserted that Rafael bore it all with patience, never complained, and was cheerful.

Undoubtedly the lack of a spiritual guide at this time adds to the suffering that the physical solitude of this period brings to Rafael, whose "life is a continual fluctuation of desolation and consolation." Yet it is right there, in desolation or consolation, that the Lord teaches him to set his heart on God alone, in sheer faith, without help or comfort from others. This spiritual solitude is very hard on Rafael, above all in moments of desolation. He well knows that God shows true love in troubles and trials, but he suffers during temptation because the Lord hides himself from him and he feels forsaken by God. At times the temptation proves so strong that he is inclined to think that he was under a delusion when he embraced the monastic life about which he was once so enthusiastic and which cost him so much in the way of self-renunciation; this kind of temptation is particularly painful for him. On one occasion he describes it very plainly:

> The other day I kept viewing everything as utterly *black*; my life, hidden and confined to the Infirmary . . . bereft of every-thing that might enable it to carry the heavy load that the Lord has dumped on me . . . Sickness, silence, desertion . . . all I know is that my interior suffering was intense. I saw myself as lacking love for God, forgotten by others, without faith, with-out light. The habit depressed me . . . I kept seeing myself as *dead while still alive* . . . the notion that I was *buried alive* obsessed me, was driving me crazy . . . at those moments I would have liked to really die . . . *but only in order to escape having to suffer* . . . Later I realized it was a temptation.

The challenge of the cross

What with all that made him suffer, a sick man living in the solitude of a cell in the Infirmary and in the solitude of his spiritual state, it is easy to understand the important place that Rafael gives to the cross in his writings at this period. It was only to be expected. Since he writes about what he is living through, he now has to write about the cross with which the Lord keeps teaching him detachment from creatures and not seeking perfec-tion except in God.

Although it is very difficult to forsake freedom in order to embrace the cross, and although very few renounce themselves in order to welcome it, Rafael has from the first embraced Christ's cross, even if subsequently, at certain moments, he may lose heart. Still, his longing for the cross does not lessen; he wants to love it madly, and asks the Lord to teach him how to do so in complete solitude from everything and everyone. At the same time, he asks to be allowed to stand always at the foot of the cross, in its shade; to make his cell there, his bed, his delight, his repose when suffering, so convinced is he that there is no better place. So he writes:

> Only lately have I come to know how pleasant the paths of Christ are, but I have always found consolation in the cross. What little I know I have learned from the cross. My prayer and meditations have always been made at the cross . . . The fact is that I know no better place nor am I able to find one . . . so, be still.

Which is why, on considering the divine school which the cross is, where alone he can learn to improve, to love the Lord, to forget himself, he arrives at the conclusion that he offends the Lord whenever he departs from it; and every day he keeps repeating the prayer, "Lord, do not allow me to depart from you."

Rafael has learned by experience how well one lives if one clings to the cross, which has become for him so great a treasure that daily he loves his cross more and more, and would not part with it for anything in the world. He would like to go crazy because of his great love for his obsession, his cross. He has found in it just what could never have been expected—his heart's desire. He does not know how to pray, does not know how to be good, has no religious spirit; all he knows is that he has a treasure that he would not exchange for anyone or anything—his cross, the cross of Jesus that is his only rest. God is so much present in it that as long as one does not love it, one neither perceives nor senses his presence. There, at the sight of the Lord's pain, there is no pain; there all else is forgotten, so much does the thought of such love prevail. Only love for Christ's cross enables one not to despair of one's own pain. For all these reasons Rafael lays his heart at the foot of the cross, and would like to cry out amid the peoples how sublime a thing love for the cross is, love that he has enjoyed and which makes him completely happy even in his exile.

Indeed, while he clings to the cross, Rafael is happy even now in a way that no one could have imagined; in love for the cross of Christ he has found true happiness. He is happy when, at the foot of the cross of Christ, he tells him of his sufferings and offers Christ his delight in being loved by him, to such an extent that he forgets the hunger that he endures and that causes him so much suffering. He is happy a thousand times over even when, in his weakness, he at times complains. Yes, he is so happy that shortly before his death he begins to be suspicious about his happiness being so great and such a contrast to all that he had suffered earlier. He writes:

> I am afraid. I distrust myself. I am very much afraid at finding myself so happy with Jesus, and only with Jesus. I have suffered so much for the last four years! I have been interiorly tormented for so long . . . that now, *on seeing that it was a necessary preparation for this* . . . I am afraid and I do not know of what!

By now Rafael is happy in a new way. The more his interior disposition changes completely, what once made him suffer makes no difference in the least to him now, as already mentioned. By now he is happy only with God and his cross, and he envies no one. He does not want worldly happiness, since he considers that it would make him wretched; rather he is completely happy in his La Trappe because he is completely wretched, a fact that at times he cannot understand, although he finds the last place to be the best.

Living in the last place

Striving to be the last except when it comes to obeying, Rafael lives out this stage of his life in the monastery, achieving thereby the third purpose he had when reentering. The Lord teaches him the path he should take, namely, "to be the last, the poor, sick Trappist oblate," one who is a nothing and a nobody, insignificant and worthless, but glad to be so. From knowing and welcoming his nothingness and worthlessness, Rafael comes to the conclusion that nothingness itself is good enough for him,

and that he is the last of all. But he considers himself the last of all
not only in the order of seniority in the community (being merely
an oblate and not a professed monk), but also, having prayed to
the Lord to teach him the path his nothingness should take, he
willingly regards himself as the last of all, counting himself the
most worldly and sin-laden. Such a view of his real self begets
in Rafael a disposition of profound humility and charity, which
he himself describes:

> Lord, at such moments I would wish to be walked on by ev-
> eryone; I feel a great love and charity for everyone; it would
> not bother me were the least of them to order me to do the
> most humiliating things . . . I see neither weakness nor
> wretchedness in anyone . . . *all I see is my baseness loved by God*
> . . . faced with that, what would I not do to imitate Him? . . .
> So [I must] dearly love my neighbor.

Knowledge of his own personal indigence as loved and par-
doned by the Lord has helped him change his attitude with regard
to the frailties of his fellow monks. Rafael himself would mention
the great miracle wrought by God on his interior disposition by
transforming it with regard to love for neighbor.[8] He used to be
so disappointed at the defects of some that he would withdraw
from dealing with them, not knowing any better because of being
alone and without a spiritual guide. But now he finds himself
full of great longing to love all in the community as Jesus himself
does, thanks to a miracle from the Lord who has led him to better self-knowledge by enabling him to see that he is the last of
all because he is nothing. But his nothingness has changed into
a treasure for Rafael, and he feels tenderness toward a brother
who has a weakness or commits a fault.

---

8. Sure enough, on leaving the monastery for the third time, he had mentioned in a letter to his uncle that he "had learned to love people just as they
are and not as I would wish they were," as already mentioned. However, later
on in the monastery, he found it difficult in practice to accept some of his fellow monks as they were; it would seem that where monks were concerned, he
tended to idealize.

Living paradoxically

Such are the dispositions with which Rafael spends his final period in the monastery; while endeavoring to live unobtrusively, doing nothing extraordinary, he keeps hiding his love for God from others. He behaves like one in the Infirmary, but with a smile on his lips, doing quite simply whatever he is asked to do, obeying promptly and keeping secret from others his longing to die clinging to the cross and to penance.

This time, too, his days pass rapidly and without his noticing, and all the more so when he passes them with the Crucified. His time is occupied with *lectio divina*,[9] with reflection, with meditation, with the choral Office, and with learning Latin. When able, he does some sweeping to help the Brother Infirmarian, or with pencil and paintbrush makes good use of a Sunday to make holy pictures, based on the Psalms that are his spiritual nourishment. Even though by now he has become used to being confined to the Infirmary, he finds it hard to have to spend two months without enjoying the open air and the sunshine, feeling rather sorry for himself on having to work in the monastery's shady chocolate factory one fine day of balmy blue sky. Later, however, remembering that he had come to the monastery to do penance, it seemed to him that God was telling him, "Courage, Rafael . . . it is all so transient . . ." and his grief left him.

At this time, Rafael often had to contend with the kind of mood swings that he mentions to the Lord: "No sooner am I flooded with deep interior bitterness than I am filled with rejoicing gladness when I think of you and of what you promise for the end of the journey." Continual change from desolation to consolation and back makes him feel that his interior is a whirlwind. At times Rafael can make neither head nor tail of it, and does not know either what he wants or what he desires, nor if he desires or wants at all. Sometimes he lives his monastic life and the desires he brought to it paradoxically. At times he thinks his heart is free from every single thing; at times he realizes that it is not. He lives stuck in the mire of his wretchedness, and at the very same time he lives only for God, athirst for him; when he sees himself as

9. Bible-based monastic reading.—Trans.

most miserable and most wretched is just when he feels he loves the Lord most. He freely asks for the cross, and then he weeps, forgetting that he has asked for it. He greatly loves God in solitude and is happy in his seclusion, but he is well aware that he is centered not in his La Trappe but in God crucified, since his life is a continual martyrdom, and at times an experience of intense blackness that makes him weep, not knowing what it is.

Reacting to what he is going through at this particular time makes Rafael sometimes feel that he would not exchange his pains for all the gold in the world, and at that very time he weeps over his troubles and his lack of consolation to such an extent as to longingly desire death in order to cease suffering; at other times he does not want to lack suffering even after death. Rafael is but living the great paradox he has already mentioned: he is completely happy in his La Trappe because he is completely wretched in it. The outside world cannot make it out and he is unable to explain it. "It is so difficult to explain why one loves suffering!" Still, he feels more intensely glad to be able to suffer for Jesus than he could ever have imagined possible, and he is ready to leave his La Trappe were God to indicate some other place where he would suffer even more, and God were to ask it of him.

He offers his life—He is promised the cowl

On February 27 an important event in Rafael's life took place. He had already offered his heart and his will to the Lord; now he offers him his life. He writes of it clearly and decisively: "Today I have offered to the Lord the one thing that remained to me . . . : my life. I have placed it at His feet, for Him to accept and to use as He likes, and to take it whenever He wants, and for whatever he likes." Until this moment Rafael would suffer when he found himself deprived of many necessary things, or noticed how he was deliberately shortening his life, or saw it as sickly and forever without relief; all that is now finished. He has offered it to God, and now it is not his own. It is for God to take care of it. For his part he will treat it as something on loan, but he will not be concerned about it. He will not be concerned in any way about his state of health; he will take what he is given, do what he is told, and obey in everything. It is for God to be responsible for what happens to him. If he wants him to have a long and pain-filled life, so be it; if he wants to take it tonight, so be it as well. For Rafael all that remains is to die whenever God wants him to do so. For his part, he would like to die forsaken by all; but above all, he would like to die of love, considering that it must be easy to die when one has God in one's heart.

Meanwhile, during Lent that year, Rafael—who as he sees it ought to be a saint and is not, and who does not want to be ungrateful or to waste time—wants little by little to die of love to all that is still in the way of his living for the Lord alone. He knew well that God dwells in a heart that is purified and detached, and that the way to holiness consists more in removing than in retaining things. In line with this, Rafael, desiring mortification and penance and longing to suffer for the Lord, one day asked the Abbot for some penance he might undertake during Lent. The Abbot not only refused but immediately added that on Easter Sunday he would give him the monastic cowl and black scapular proper to professed monks.[10] The immediate effect of this news was to make Rafael very glad, since for some time he had been daydreaming about the cowl. However, his second reaction was to admit—he knew himself so well!—that this was just personal vanity, and all that God was asking of him was love and a spirit of self-sacrifice. Moreover, God is not in the monastic habit or hairdo, but in a heart that is completely detached. Having gotten rid of worldly notions, Rafael was thrilled to discover that God alone filled his life. And this is what God kept teaching him in his solitude and distress, in sheer faith, in the abyss of his nothingness and in the arms of the cross.

Under the influence of and the desire for God

So he gets over his silly and somewhat childish gladness at the prospect of receiving the cowl. Rafael can afford to make light of the monastic cowl and coiffure since he wants to make his cell in the heart of Christ, living all alone with God and stripped of all else. What he regards as excessive esteem makes him afraid,

10. Such bestowal of the cowl on a mere oblate had no precedent in the history of the monastery of San Isidoro.

for he is glad to live unknown, and even thinks that it would be still better if he forgot about himself.

Making his love his one and only reason for living, he spends his days contentedly and happily, and he knows from his own experience that for one who loves God nothing is difficult. The Lord has done great things for him, not least by enabling him to be so detached. Rafael has done nothing for him, and nonetheless the Lord's mercy is so great! He feels himself loved, guided, supported by God who knows what he is and how he is, and who makes nothing of Rafael's great deficiency in reciprocating his love. And yet, in spite of what he was, of the wretch that he is,[11] despite everything, Rafael is aware of having God, who watches over him beyond all that anyone could imagine. This is why he is happier each day in his complete surrender into God's hands, so sure is he that God "does everything for our salvation."

Rafael is forever making a start at serving God, and he sees that, in spite of his good intentions and desires, he does nothing. That which he wants to offer to the Lord he no longer possesses, since he has already offered it all to him. He experiences not only the divine miracle that the Lord has wrought within him, but that he continues to influence him interiorly. He feels that the Lord is withdrawing him interiorly from everything, separating him from futility and creatures, and enabling him to discover that in God there is true peace. In fact, by now creatures have no message for Rafael; as his interior disposition changes, they are mere sounds to him. Only in silence, free from everything and everyone, does he find what he is looking for; he wants neither to know nor to listen to anything; why, he senses that the Lord is withdrawing him even from his family, and he is increasingly convinced that in God alone is all that is necessary.

Thanks to this latest spiritual purification, Rafael realizes that only in God does he find what he is looking for. Not finding in

---

11. At this very time Rafael is living at a very high level of union with God. As a result he has a strong sense of being a sinner, which he describes in terms that are more severe than ever before, like, "My frightful sins, my faults, my ingratitude, my misery, my sins, my *utter wickedness*, which I still need to bewail for a long time here on earth." Yet as we have said above (p. 48, n. 6), those who knew him well and knew his life have affirmed that he never lost his baptismal innocence.

others what he at one time thought to find no longer matters; it is over and done with. He experiences the boundless gladness of possessing the Truth, of finding himself possessing and possessed by God. His only desire now is to love the Lord thoroughly, the Lord who in his boundless love comforts Rafael's heart that thirsts for him; and Rafael would die of grief were he to find that he loves someone more than he loves the Lord.

Nonetheless, Rafael knows that the full possession of God is not possible in this present life, which is why he feels tired when he sees himself a stranger and pilgrim on earth, in this exile that is a hindrance to complete joy in the Lord. How is it possible to really live when one waits for what he is waiting for? No wonder he finds living so difficult! He is tired of such living and longs to fly away to God. He is in a hurry to be with the Lord, and begs Him not to delay, for he has an intimation that everything down here will be over for him soon.[12] Still, while on the one hand he longs for the finish, on the other hand it is all the same to him, for now his whole ambition is to fulfill God's will.

At this very point in his spiritual development, when he wants God alone to be his life and to take him soon, Rafael does nevertheless remember the apostolic motive that brought him back to the monastery. On Holy Thursday, happy to be united with the Lord's suffering on the cross, he begs the Lord to share with the many needy in all the world all that he, the Lord, gives to him. He begs the Lord to listen to his supplication, pointing out all that he would have him remedy: Spain, the Civil War, his brothers and sister, the many friends whom he loves, his parents . . . yes, even in exchange for his life, he tells the Lord, "Take me and give yourself to the world." And the Lord listens to him.

He receives the cowl. He dies

As promised, on Easter Sunday Rafael received the cowl. He candidly admits that in this connection he had succumbed to vanity, and this leads him to ask the Lord for mercy, to grant him holy fear of God and to fill his heart with love. If only he had as

---

12. On March 28, Rafael thought that his life would be over soon, and he was to die less than a month later.

much love for God as he has cloth to spare in the wide sleeves of the cowl! He does not know what to do with them! Which does not matter—to be dressed one way or another, to be here or there, is vanity of vanities.

On this same day, Easter Sunday, April 17, he wrote to his family, telling them that he feels happy, that his days, as usual, go by without his noticing it, that he hopes the Civil War will soon be over and they can come to visit him. This is the last letter that Rafael ever wrote. He would die nine days later, without ever seeing his family again, except for his father.

His father arrived at the monastery on Easter Thursday morning, April 21, for a visit. Rafael, dressed like a proper monk in white cowl and black scapular, met him. Never had his father seen him with better color in his cheeks, with such a sparkle in his eyes. He simply radiated happiness and peace. With his usual cheerfulness and the humor and smile that were characteristic of him, he said to his father: "Here you have a Brother with a lot of cloth. I do not know what to do with the sleeves." They went for a walk in the garden, and had a chat with the Abbot, who had plans for new farm buildings which Rafael was expected to design. The Abbot told Rafael's father that his son would soon have enough Latin, and then he would straight away receive ordination to the priesthood. When he asked Rafael if he thought this a good idea, if he did not desire to be ordained, Rafael replied that he was indifferent as to whether he was ordained or not. Indeed, he had reached such a degree of indifference that by then it was all the same to him. All he wanted was whatever God wanted; but he himself was convinced that he would never become a priest because he would die before then.

As a witness at the Process stated:

> Once the superiors decided that he was to be a priest, I was assigned to give him Latin classes. When encouraging him to study Latin, which he found difficult, I would tell him to think of the priesthood. His reply was, "Look, Father, I will study Latin with you because the superiors command me to do so, and I should obey, but I will not become a priest. All I ask of God is that they give me the Cistercian cowl before I die."[13]

13. His brother, Leopoldo, also testified during the Process, "Not long before he died, he told me that he would die soon and that he had only a few months left to live."

In fact, after receiving the cowl, Rafael was already close to death. He bade farewell that Easter Thursday to his father, who had not the slightest inkling that he was embracing his son for the last time. The following day Rafael took to his bed with a high fever.

His condition did not seem all that serious, but he was in fact dying. He was noticeably tired and failing. He was often seen leaving his room in the Infirmary as he frequently needed to pass water and his sugar-filled urine caused him intense pain. His high fever went higher still, and led to intermittent delirium and long periods of unconsciousness. "Do not be frightened if I become delirious," he would say with a smile to the monks who took care of him. Delirious and suffering from the most severe pain, he would speak incoherently between the violent convulsions resulting from his illness. Once critically grave moments passed he would recover his serenity and complete resignation; he had longed to have the greatest possible strength to suffer, considering that all our sufferings are as nothing compared to those of the crucified Jesus; and he had once remarked, "Which of us has reason to complain at having to suffer?"

Rafael never uttered a single word of complaint about the symptoms of his sickness: the fierce hunger that devoured him and the unquenchable thirst he had to endure. All these sufferings seemed little enough to one who had said, "It is pleasant to suffer, beyond the help of others, clinging to the cross of Christ." And indeed he never let go of Christ's cross as long as there was life in him; such was his fortitude, to which several bore witness during the Process, that "he even went so far as to tell the Infirmarian to pay no heed when he heard the buzzer, it merely reflected the stress of his illness."

Particular fortitude reaching to heroism was evident in what happened some forty-eight hours before his death, as mentioned in the Process as well. During the night of Low Sunday, Rafael, thinking that he was alone in his Infirmary cell, got up with difficulty from his bed and stumbled, pressing hands that shook with fever along the walls, to a cold water tap at the end of the corridor. Burning thirst was killing him. He put his glowing lips to the cold metal, but did not drink. He preferred to die of thirst like the Lord. The Infirmarian—Brother Constantine, not Brother

Domingo, who had been inconsiderate towards him—who had witnessed that silent self-denial, accosted him when he returned to his cell, and kindly pointed out his not drinking, but Rafael's answer was, "Do not worry, Brother, I am well aware of what I do."

Rafael's condition deteriorated rapidly. At dawn on Monday, April 25, looking the worse for his great suffering, he received Extreme Unction, being unable to receive the Viaticum. His condition became frightening and desperate; he was unable to speak, and scarcely understood what was said to him.

At dawn on Tuesday, Rafael regained his senses for a short time and faced his death with full consciousness. He recognized the Father Master, who encouraged him to hope to live. Rafael calmly and quietly replied, "My end is near. Soon I will make my way to heaven." Toward six in the morning his agony began. While the Commendation of the Soul was being recited for him, Rafael suffered a strong convulsion that for a few moments very much distorted his face. Then it returned to its normal appearance, and with quiet peacefulness and a smile on his lips, as if enjoying a pleasant dream, he breathed his last. It was April 26, 1938. A few days earlier Rafael had completed his twenty-seventh year.

IX

CONCLUSION

No doubt Brother Rafael's life was uncomplicated on the whole, but it was also unique, if only because of the many times he returned to the Cistercian monastery of San Isidoro. What could be called the first stage of Rafael's life does not differ all that much from that of so many others who have, like him, embraced Trappist life. He was born into a Christian family, in which he received the good formation that was further enhanced by the one he later received at various Jesuit colleges. Naturally kind-hearted, artistically inclined, and spiritually perceptive, in the early youth that followed a happy childhood Rafael had already begun to live an earnest Christian life. His relations with his uncle and aunt, the Duke and Duchess of Maqueda, helped him advance in the spiritual life and led him to visit his La Trappe for the first time. This would decidedly change the course of his life.

Like many another young man, once Rafael found that the values of monastic life suited him, he decided to become a monk. This meant that he had to renounce the comfortable lifestyle that his family's wealth made possible, and also the course in architecture that he had begun. No matter, his La Trappe for him was everything, and he would have renounced anything and everything to live there.

Thus far Rafael's life is rather similar to that of other contemporaries of his who entered a monastery. Possibly in Rafael's case the renunciation was greater, since, thanks to the resources of his family, his life in the outside world provided him with so much; but in fact monastic life demands a similar renunciation from everyone: one must leave what one has in order to take on the observances of a monastery.

It would also seem that Rafael's first months in the monastery were, externally at least, like those of his fellow novices. Still, his already amazing spiritual life must not be forgotten, and now he gave himself wholeheartedly to traveling the path he had discovered, for he regarded it as meant by God for him. He felt at home, happy in his La Trappe, until his unexpected illness forced him to leave the monastery. But the Abbot when bidding him farewell told him that he must return. Perhaps it was at that point that Rafael's life began to indicate that it included an unusual spiritual itinerary. He had thought that his renunciation of everything had been final, and suddenly he found that the Lord was taking him out of the monastery because of his illness. He suffered but he accepted God's will, which would make use of diabetes to liberate his disposition, since until then he had been much attached to everything that his La Trappe offered and meant.

The months went by and Rafael was not cured of the illness he had come to regard as a blessing from God. Nonetheless, he still felt called to Trappist life. However, his continuing ill health made him realize that he had to give up the idea of becoming a full-fledged monk. During his stay in the monastery, having come across the Statute on Oblates, he considered that this was the way he was called to live in the monastery. By now he had no wish to return to the monastery for the sake of any more or less romantic idea, not even for the sake of the perfectly lawful ambition of becoming a professed monk; the only reason he wanted to return to the monastery was to love God and his neighbor. His stay in the outside world had changed his disposition by detaching it from earlier notions. He thought that his vocation was to be an oblate in the monastery, humbly accepting all that that implied for one of high social standing, who had had every prospect of success in the outside world. The superiors of the monastery granted him readmission as an oblate.

So Rafael entered his La Trappe the second time, and stayed until called up by his country, but only to be declared useless for military service. But he did not make his departure from the monastery for the Civil War a reason for staying on with his family: the monastery continued to draw him and he returned to it. However, two months later he had to leave it once again because of a serious recurrence of his illness, which had compelled him to live very much apart in the Infirmary of the monastery before his departure, an experience which he had found rather painful.

Ten months later, Rafael reentered the monastery for the last time, and died shortly after. This time he entered in order to accomplish in the monastery his vocation to love God on the cross and in self-sacrifice, and so make the best use of the life span God gave him.

All through this biography an effort has been made to explicate Rafael's interior experience amid all the to and fro that filled his life. And in this conclusion it seems good to focus particularly on something that is really remarkable in Rafael's life: his tenacious constancy in reentering his La Trappe, despite indications that he had no monastic vocation. With even the most elementary discernment in the matter of a vocation, it would seem that one should not follow an attraction to a calling for which one lacks the necessary aptitude. Rafael, on account of his illness, certainly lacked a necessary aptitude for monastic life. But he was able to accept the condition of an oblate, which is provided for those who feel called to live in a monastery although unable to follow the full observance of the Rule. This was what he proposed to do at his first reentry, and it was accepted by the superiors of the monastery.

Still, how to interpret Rafael's subsequently desiring reentry when he was, in any case, advancing in purification and detachment from everything, and had reached his "God alone" stance? What made him continue to desire the monastery despite his poor health? He had experienced God in his La Trappe, experienced the great change that God had wrought in him there, and he wanted to return. Moreover, his spiritual development had modified the motivation for his vocation, and it focused now on the cross and on self-sacrifice, which he thought he could fulfill better in the monastery. His desire to reenter his La Trappe was no longer for La Trappe as such, since he was unable to keep its Rule. The will of God had become his one and only rule, and he planned to fulfill it by his third reentry to the monastery as an oblate.

Rafael was convinced that the Lord was calling him to the monastery. Since his illness made no difference in the case of an oblate, it was not in any way a decisive element by which to

discern his reentering or not. He had always been certain that
he would die in his La Trappe, and had always thought that the
Lord was calling him there, no matter what. Rafael, who found
nothing fully worthwhile in the outside world, sensed with a kind
of spiritual instinct an attraction to life in the monastery,[1] while
well aware that he would never be able to live the full community
life. Perhaps he was unable to prove his strong desire to live in
his La Trappe by positive signs, but this did not mean that it was
not the result of the action of the Spirit on him interiorly, giving
his attraction the force of a vocation, not only intellectually but
emotionally, that drove him towards monastic life, towards living in a monastery.

This seems to be borne out by the monks who knew Rafael and testified during the Process about his reentries into the
monastery. They all agreed that he returned in order to fulfill his
vocation, because of his longing to live at his La Trappe whether
he was well or ill, and because he wanted to die there, even if
only as an oblate. One witness said, "He had a crazy longing to
return." And, it may be added, he did so willingly, because he
perceived that God was calling him there, and what he wanted
was to fulfill God's will, although he was well aware what returning to the monastery would mean for him. Nonetheless, in the
words of a witness, "he was simply full of the particular grace
that God grants to one called to be a Trappist."

Rafael's friend and confidant before he entered for the first
time stated during the Process, "His desire to return to his La
Trappe must in no way be regarded as if he was obeying any other
reasons except those proper to a genuinely-felt vocation." Moreover, Rafael always depended on being accepted by the superiors
of the monastery. Not only that, he himself expressly requested
the Abbot to consider his case before God, and find out whether
his vocation as an oblate was God-given or not. By welcoming
Rafael the superiors approved of his desires, and acknowledged
and accepted his vocation as a fact.

What reasons persuaded the Abbot to welcome Rafael again
and again to the monastery? Frankly, they are now unknown, not

---

1. The normal process of the call of God manifests itself through *taste* or
distaste, or if one prefers, through consolation or desolation.

being mentioned in any document. The most likely reason would seem to be that the Abbot in his dealings with Rafael came to know his far from ordinary greatness of soul. Proof of this would seem to be that he wished Rafael to return when he first left the monastery, a desire he expressed to him openly; and, in addition to welcoming his requests to return, despite his illness and the Civil War, he wanted to get him ordained to the priesthood and actually gave him the monastic cowl, an unusual thing to do at San Isidoro. This last detail looks like an acknowledgement by the Abbot of Rafael's virtues.

It seems right to conclude this point by stating that Rafael returned repeatedly to the monastery in answer to God's particular call to him; a special call, outside the usual norms. He was not meant to live the life *of* his La Trappe; he was meant to live *in* his La Trappe, and, it may be added, to suffer and die in his La Trappe. His was an exceptional vocation, but it was acknowledged and accepted by those responsible in the monastery, even if it meant nonconformity with the normal life prescribed by the Rule. And it was accepted above all by Rafael himself, who answered it, fully aware that by going to the monastery he was shortening a life already impaired by illness, which is why it seems right to regard him as a "martyr to his vocation." And doubtless, a martyr to his love, the love that killed him, just as he himself had desired and declared over and over again.

Saint John of the Cross says that people who have reached intimate union with God do not leave this life because of illness or old age (even if they die of illness or of old age), but by the force of their love.[2] So, although the death certificate signed by the Abbot states that "a diabetic coma" was what snatched Rafael's life away so soon, all those in the know were quite sure that it was more the fire of his charity and of his great love for God than his illness that did it. And thus the parchment that was kept in the casket containing Rafael's remains after their exhumation and removal in 1965 stated, "He breathed his last consumed by love for God." It would seem that Rafael at the end of his days could have made his own those lines from Saint John of the Cross that

---

2. *The Living Flame of Love*, Stanza 1,30.

he was undoubtedly aware of and that reflect so well the high
altitude of his spiritual flight:

> In a wonderful way I flew
> A thousand flights in one,
> For by heaven-sent hope is won
> Whatever is expected and true;
> I gambled on this one chance,
> And my hope did not belie,
> Since I went so high, so high,
> That I up to the prey did advance[3]

In view of what his life was like it seems right to apply to him
these words of the Book of Wisdom: "With him early achievement
counted for long apprenticeship; so well did the Lord love him
that from a corrupt world he granted him swift release" (Wis
4:13-14). Yes, Rafael was a man pleasing to God, one whose purpose was to love God as fully as possible, God alone, as expressed
in his oft-repeated cry: GOD ALONE! Like all the saints Rafael
was a "friend of God," which was acknowledged by the Church
at his recent beatification on September 27, 1992.

Certainly nothing essential can be added to the genuine glory
of any follower of Jesus. The follower who has entrusted his life
into God's hands enters definitively after death into the depths
of the divine mystery that during this present life was passion-
ately sought and glimpsed in love. Still, for us who are as yet
the Pilgrim Church, it is a great joy and truly glorious to be able
to acknowledge and proclaim, with the authoritative guarantee
of the Church, the sanctification and transformation, in Christ
through the Spirit, achieved in the outstanding children of the
Church, and in this case, in our Brother Rafael. This acknowledgement is endorsed by the words used at the beatification
ceremony by John Paul II. They are reproduced here as the best
ending for this book:

> Knowing the desire of our brother . . . Ricardo Blázquez Pérez,
> bishop of Palencia . . . and of many others of our brother
> bishops, and of a great number of the faithful, having listened
> to the advice of the Congregation for the Causes of the Saints,

3. Poem 11,4, in Spanish edition.

with our own Apostolic Authority, we grant that the Venera-
ble Servant of God, Rafael Arnáiz Barón . . . be called Blessed
and that his Feast may be celebrated every year in the places
and in the manner prescribed by Church Law on the day of
his passing to heaven—April 26 . . . In the Name of the Father and of the Son and of the Holy Spirit.

X

CHRONOLOGY OF THE LIFE OF BLESSED RAFAEL

1911   April 9—Rafael is born in Burgos.

1911   April 21—he receives Baptism in the church of Santa Agueda, and is named Rafael Arturo José.

1913   December 1—he receives Confirmation in the Niño Jesús school at Burgos.

1919   October 25—he receives Holy Communion for the first time in the chapel of the Visitandines at Burgos.

1920   October—he enters Jesuit La Merced school as a day student; after two months, however, he has to absent himself because of illness.

1921   October—he returns to school at the beginning of the term.

1922   Rafael and his family move to Oviedo city.

1923   He continues his education at Jesuit San Ignacio school in Oviedo.

1926   He begins taking lessons in painting apart from but without interrupting his school classes.

1930   After taking a degree at Oviedo University on April 15, he is admitted to the College of Architecture in Madrid on April 16.

1930   September 21—he makes his first visit to the Cistercian monastery of San Isidoro de Dueñas.

1931 February—he is admitted as an active member of Nocturnal Adoration at Oviedo.

1932 June 17–26—he makes a retreat at the Cistercian monastery of San Isidoro.

1932 September 17—for the sake of his studies, Rafael settles at Madrid, where he remains until his compulsory military service.

1933 January 25–July 26—he does his military service.

1934 January 15—Rafael enters Novitiate at the monastery of San Isidoro and remains for four months of full observance.

1934 May 26—gravely ill with diabetes and at the orders of his superiors, he returns home.

1936 January 11—he reenters the monastery, but as an oblate, not being fit to continue his novitiate or take monastic vows because of his illness.

1936 September 29—he leaves the monastery with other young monks when called up on account of the Civil War.

1936 December 6—he returns to the monastery after being declared totally useless for military service at the battle front.

1937 February 7—the superiors send him home again owing to deterioration in his condition and because of the difficulties created in the monastery by the Civil War.

1937 December 15—he returns for the last time to the monastery.

1938 April 26—he dies with a reputation for sanctity; on the following day, after a solemn funeral, his remains are buried in the cemetery of the community.